Grammar in use
Intermediate

WITH ANSWERS

William R. Smalzer
with Raymond Murphy

CAMBRIDGE
UNIVERSITY PRESS

PUBLISHED BY THE PRESS SYNDICATE OF THE UNIVERSITY OF CAMBRIDGE
The Pitt Building, Trumpington Street, Cambridge, United Kingdom

CAMBRIDGE UNIVERSITY PRESS
The Edinburgh Building, Cambridge CB2 2RU, UK
40 West 20th Street, New York, NY 10011–4211, USA
477 Williamstown Road, Port Melbourne, VIC 3207, Australia
Ruiz de Alarcón 13, 28014 Madrid, Spain
Dock House, The Waterfront, Cape Town 8001, South Africa

http://www.cambridge.org

First published 2003

Printed in the United States of America

Typeface Sabon (Adobe®) System QuarkXPress®   [AH]

A catalog record for this book is available from the British Library
Library of Congress Cataloging in Publication data available

ISBN 0 521 79720 9 Workbook (with answers)
ISBN 0 521 79719 5 Workbook (without answers)
ISBN 0 521 62598 X Student's Book (with answers)
ISBN 0 521 62597 1 Student's Book (without answers)

Illustrations: Randy Jones and Susann Ferris Jones
Art direction, book design, and layout services: Adventure House, NYC

Contents

To the Student

Grammar in Use Intermediate Workbook provides you with additional practice in North American English grammar, building on the grammar points presented and practiced in the *Grammar in Use Intermediate* student's book. It offers additional exercises on difficult grammar points and a variety of exercise types. The workbook will be useful in helping you apply what you have already learned in the student's book.

The workbook covers the same grammar points as the student's book and in the same order. The types of exercises in the workbook are often different from those in the student's book, however. This way you can apply what you have learned in a slightly different way. The exercises in this workbook will also help you understand how the grammar points in one unit of the student's book are related to the grammar in other units. You may be called on to use several different grammar structures in one exercise.

In general, workbook exercises will require you to read longer passages and write longer responses than the exercises in the student's book. In some exercises, you will rewrite whole sentences using different grammar forms but keeping the same meaning. In other exercises, you will read paragraphs and fill in blanks with correct forms, or answer questions that call on your understanding of grammar. In review exercises, you will have the chance to use your own ideas to complete or rewrite sentences.

Level

Like the student's book, the *Grammar in Use Intermediate Workbook* is intended mainly for intermediate students (students who have already studied the basic grammar of English). The book is not suitable for beginning learners. However, advanced learners who have problems with grammar will also find the book useful.

How the workbook is organized

There are 156 exercises covering all 133 units in the student's book. One exercise in the workbook may cover the grammar in one, two, or three units in the student's book, however. Each workbook exercise has a heading that indicates the units of the student's book that are covered in that exercise. Workbook exercises are grouped into sections, according to the sections in the student's book (see the Contents). At the end of each section there are review exercises.

How to use the workbook

Use the workbook only after you have completed the corresponding units in the student's book. If you have trouble with the exercises on the right-hand pages of the student's book, review the left-hand pages of those units. Then do the workbook exercises for those units.

Checking Your Work

After you have done an exercise or group of exercises in the workbook, check your answers in the Answer Key at the back of the book. You can use the Answer Key in several different ways:

Students working alone

Check your answers at the back of the book.

Students working in pairs

Student A: Read your answers to Student B, who will tell you if they are correct.
Student B: Refer to the key as you listen to Student A answer each item. In case of errors, try to help your partner find the correct solution rather than just reading it.

Groups of four or more (working in pairs)

Work with a partner on an exercise. Decide on your answers together. When you finish, compare answers with another pair of students. Discuss any differences. Finally, check the Answer Key together.

Groups of four or more (working with a leader)

Choose a leader. The leader opens the book to the Answer Key. The other group members take turns reading their answers. For each answer, group members compare their own solutions to the one they heard, discussing any differences. The leader, after listening to all the other members, reads the correct response.

If you do not understand an answer in the Answer Key, ask your teacher or someone who knows English well to explain the answer to you. The exercises that ask you to use your own ideas usually have sample answers in the Answer Key. Of course, your answers may be different. If you are studying in a class, your teacher may check your answers to those exercises.

To the Teacher

Grammar in Use Intermediate Workbook provides exercises to reinforce and extend the grammar lessons presented and practiced in the *Grammar in Use Intermediate* student's book. An exercise in the workbook typically covers more than one unit in the student's book, in order to help students consolidate their knowledge of related grammar points. Thus, workbook exercises are often slightly more challenging than exercises in the student's book, in addition to having more varied formats.

The workbook covers all 133 units in the student's book. At the beginning of every workbook exercise is a heading which indicates the titles and numbers of the relevant units in the student's book. Intended to supplement the student's book, workbook exercises should be done after the relevant units in the student's book have been completed. Exercises in the workbook are organized into sections, corresponding to the sections in the Contents in the *Grammar in Use Intermediate* student's book. Review exercises can be found at the end of each section.

This book will be most useful for students at the intermediate and upper-intermediate levels. It will also be useful for more advanced students who need further practice on particular grammar points. It is not suitable for students at the beginning or low-intermediate levels. Like the student's book, the workbook can be used by whole classes, by individual students needing extra help, or for independent study. Many of the exercises lend themselves better to writing than to oral work. These exercises may be done independently, or by students working together in the classroom.

This self-study edition of the workbook contains an answer key. Exercises that ask students to use their own ideas usually have sample answers, but students' actual answers may of course be different. You might want to look over student answers to such exercises at intervals, or have students compare answers in groups. A classroom edition of the *Grammar in Use Intermediate Workbook* without an answer key is also available.

WORKBOOK

Grammar
in use
Intermediate

EXERCISE 1

Present Continuous (*I am doing*)

A. Complete B's answers. Use an expression from the box in the present continuous.

paint the bedrooms	not get better	improve all the time	study law
take a shower	~~visit her~~	have a good time	make a salad

A	B
1. Why isn't Claire studying?	Because some friends _are visiting her_____.
2. Why is the doctor worried about your leg?	Because it _____.
3. Why are you cutting tomatoes?	Because I _____.
4. Why are the Lee children sleeping in the living room?	Because their parents _____.
5. Why doesn't Bill answer the telephone?	He's in the bathroom. He _____.
6. It's late. Why don't you want to go home?	It's a nice party and I _____.
7. Is your sister in medical school?	No. She _____.
8. Are you pleased with your English?	Yes. It _____.

B. Write complete sentences for questions 1 to 4. Use words from the question and your answer above.

1. _Claire isn't studying because some friends are visiting her._____

2. _____ worried about my leg because it

   _____.

3. I _____ because _____

   _____.

4. _____ because _____

   _____.

Simple Present (*I do*)

Write complete sentences to answer the questions. Use the simple present and a phrase from the box.

her older sister	in the library	swim in a pool every morning	~~outside on the balcony~~
work in a bank	not like him	look angry today	usually drive his car
not drink coffee	once or twice a week		

1. *A:* Where do Mr. and Mrs. White eat in the summer?

   B: *They eat outside on the balcony.* _____

2. *A:* What does Al do for exercise?

   B: He _____ .

3. *A:* Where does Sarah usually study?

   B: She _____ .

4. *A:* Who takes care of little Sally Smith after school?

   B: _____

5. *A:* What does Margaret do?

   B: _____

6. *A:* Would you like a cup of coffee?

   B: No thanks. I _____ .

7. *A:* Why doesn't Amy talk to Ben?

   B: _____

8. *A:* How does Bill get to work?

   B: _____

9. *A:* Why don't you want to talk to the boss?

   B: She _____ .

10. *A:* How often do you exercise?

    B: _____

Simple Present (*I do*)

Complete B's answers. Use the simple present tense.

<table>
<tr><th>A</th><th>B</th></tr>
<tr>
<td>1. Is Ben having rice and beans for dinner again?</td>
<td><u>Yes, he has rice and beans for dinner</u>
_____ two or three times a week.</td>
</tr>
<tr>
<td>2. Are you feeling dizzy* again?</td>
<td>Yes, I _____
_____ almost every morning.</td>
</tr>
<tr>
<td>3. Is it raining again?</td>
<td>Yes, _____
_____ a lot here.</td>
</tr>
<tr>
<td>4. Are you changing jobs again?</td>
<td>_____
_____ a lot.</td>
</tr>
<tr>
<td>5. Is the president traveling abroad again?</td>
<td>_____
_____ pretty often.</td>
</tr>
<tr>
<td>6. Are the Johnsons moving again?</td>
<td>_____
_____ every year or two.</td>
</tr>
<tr>
<td>7. Is Jill washing her windows again?</td>
<td>_____
_____ every month.</td>
</tr>
<tr>
<td>8. Are you having trouble with your car again?</td>
<td>_____
_____ all the time.</td>
</tr>
<tr>
<td>9. Is Mark cooking fish for dinner again?</td>
<td>_____
_____ once a week.</td>
</tr>
<tr>
<td>10. Are the Molinas watching soap operas* on TV again?</td>
<td>_____
_____ every afternoon.</td>
</tr>
</table>

* dizzy: *feeling as if everything near is spinning or turning*
* soap opera: *a TV drama, with a continuing story, about the lives and problems of a group of characters*

EXERCISE 4

Present Continuous and Simple Present (*I am doing* and *I do*)

Put the verbs in the correct tense, the present continuous or the simple present.

1. *Jerry*: Nice to meet you, Mr. Green. I'm a student at the university. (you / do) And what
   _do you do_____ ?

   Mr. Green: (not work) I'm an engineer, but I _____ right now.

2. *Mr. Smith*: (he / do) Where's Jim? _____ his homework in his room?

   Mrs. Smith: (talk) No, he _____ to a friend on the phone.

3. (go out) We _____ for dinner now. Would you like to go with us?

4. *A:* *(on a bus)* _____ (you / take) this bus to work often?

   B: (usually / get) No, I _____ a ride from a friend. (not / drive) But my

   friend _____ this week because his car is at the mechanic's.

5. I'm sorry I can't accept your invitation to dinner. (visit) My parents

   _____ from Chicago this week.

6. I'm afraid I disagree with you. (not / flow) The Mississippi River _____
   into the Atlantic Ocean.

7. (you / shout) Why _____ ? Are you angry about something?

8. *A:* (get) It _____ late. (you / want) _____
   to go home?
   B: Sure, let's go.

9. *Eric*: It's only 6:30. (you / usually / leave) _____ the house this
   early in the morning?

   Neighbor: No. (leave) I _____ early today for an appointment
   before work.

10. *A:* Should we invite Margaret to dinner?

    B: No, let's not. (always / complain) She _____ about something. (not

    want) I _____ to listen to that all evening!

11. Whose umbrella is this? (it / belong) _____ to you, Sarah?

Present Continuous and Simple Present (*I am doing* and *I do*)

Put the verb in the correct form, the present continuous or the simple present.

1. I don't know why Hannah _____*is being*_____ (be) so difficult. She
   _____*is*_____ (be) usually very nice.

2. I _____ (make) a salad for lunch today, but I
   _____ (need) some tomatoes from the store.

3. _____ you _____ (see) the parking space over
   there? Why don't we park the car there?

4. My friend Paul _____ (be) very interesting. I _____
   (think) you'll like him.

5. *A:* (*at a party*) _____ you _____ (have)
   a good time?

   B: Yes. I _____ (love) parties.

6. This soup _____ (taste) better than it _____ (look).

7. When it _____ (be) hot outside, I _____ (prefer)
   to stay inside.

8. My sister _____ (think) of going to medical school because she
   _____ (want) to help sick people.

9. *A:* What _____ this word _____ (mean)?

   B: I _____ (have) no idea.

10. This salad _____ (belong) in the refrigerator because it
    _____ (contain) mayonnaise.

11. Stop acting like a child. You _____ (not / realize) how foolish you
    _____ (be).

12. (*at a coffee shop*) _____ you _____ (use) this
    chair, or can I take it?

Simple Past (*I did*)

Use the words in parentheses to write sentences in the simple past. Some are questions.

1. (they / go / for a walk)

   They went for a walk.

2. (you / do / your exercises / this morning?)

   Did you do your exercises this morning?

3. (I / not / have / time / to visit my parents yesterday)

   I didn't have time to visit my parents yesterday.

4. (I / forget / his name)

   _____

5. (you / see / the sunset last night?)

   _____

6. (the baby / not / eat / all her breakfast)

   _____

7. (you / be / on time for work yesterday?)

   _____

8. (they / not / sell / their house for a good price)

   _____

9. (you / spend / too much money on your haircut)

   _____

10. (Amy / lose / her ring, but she / find / it)

    _____

11. (How / Ann / catch / a cold?)

    _____

12. (Martin / not / teach / last night / because it / be / a holiday)

    _____

13. (the book / cost / a lot, but / I buy / it anyway)

    _____

14. (anyone / get hurt / in the accident?)

    _____

EXERCISE 7

Past Continuous (*I was doing*)

Respond to A as shown. Use the past continuous.

A	B
1. John is studying law.	Really? *He wasn't studying law the last time I saw him.*
2. Tom's baby is walking now.	Really? She _____ the last time I saw her.
3. I'm working for a computer company now.	Really? You _____ you.
4. The Johnsons are taking a Chinese cooking class.	Really? They _____
5. My brother exercises five days a week now.	Really? _____
6. We are thinking of moving to Toronto.	Really? _____
7. Carol makes commercials* for TV.	Really? _____
8. George is having trouble at work.	Really? _____
9. My wife and I are talking about adopting* a baby.	Really? _____
10. I work at home two days a week now.	Really? _____
11. Brad and his wife are having problems with their children.	Really? _____

* commercial: *a paid advertisement on TV or radio*
* adopt: *to accept someone else's child into a family through a legal process*

EXERCISE 8

Simple Past (*I did*)
Past Continuous (*I was doing*)

Look at the illustration of an accident. Then complete the passage describing it. Put the verbs in the correct tense, the simple past or the past continuous.

intersection

I 1) ___saw___ (see) an accident while I 2) ___was walking___ (walk) to work this morning. The accident, between a blue car and a white car, 3) _____ (happen) because the driver of the white car 4) _____ (not see) the stop sign. The driver of the blue car 5) _____ (slow) down and 6) _____ (stop) at the sign. The driver of the white car 7) _____ (not notice) the stop sign because she 8) _____ (talk) to a passenger in her car. For some reason, the passenger 9) _____ (sit) in the back seat, and the driver 10) _____ (turn) around once or twice to look at her.

The white car 11) _____ (drive) into the intersection while the blue car 12) _____ (cross) it. The driver of the white car 13) _____ (try) to stop, but it 14) _____ (be) too late. She 15) _____ (hit) the front of the blue car. Fortunately, no one 16) _____ (be) hurt, probably because at the moment of the crash, both cars 17) _____ (move) slowly. After the accident, the drivers of both cars 18) _____ (get out) and 19) _____ (check) their vehicles*. They 20) _____ (speak) to each other briefly to make sure that no one 21) _____ (have) a serious injury. Five minutes later, the police 22) _____ (arrive) and 23) _____ (make) an accident report. Although it all 24) _____ (happen) very quickly, I 25) _____ (think) about it all day at work.

* vehicles: *cars, buses, and trucks*

Read the passage about twins*. Then complete the passage with the verbs in parentheses in the simple or continuous form of the present or past tense.

Ted and Ralph 1) *are* (be) twin brothers who 2) *married* (marry) twin sisters, Cindy and Sarah. All four 3) _____ (go) to high school together, but the girls 4) _____ (attend) a different college from the boys. The two couples 5) _____ (get) married on the same day a year after graduating from college. Cindy and Sarah's father 6) _____ (be) happy when they 7) _____ (ask) him to hold just one wedding for both of them. He and his wife 8) _____ (have) three younger daughters, and they will probably have to pay for their weddings, too.

The couples 9) _____ (be) happily married. They 10) _____ (live) on the same street in similar houses and 11) _____ (visit) each other often. This is good, because twins 12) _____ (be) unusually close* to each other, psychologists* say, and usually 13) _____ (spend) more time together than other brothers and sisters do. Both couples 14) _____ (plan) to wait a while before they have children because they want to work and establish* their careers first. Since they all 15) _____ (grow) up in big families and 16) _____ (enjoy) it, they want to have children.

Ted and Ralph 17) _____ (own) a small computer business together. The idea for their own business 18) _____ (come) to them while they 19) _____ (work) for another company in town. It's a young company, but they 20) _____ (do) well because they do good work and 21) _____ (know) a lot of people in town. Cindy and Sarah are dentists and have their own dental clinic. They 22) _____ (not have) a lot of patients right now, but their business 23) _____ (grow). They 24) _____ (borrow) money from their father to start the clinic two years ago. They 25) _____ (want) to be independent, so they 26) _____ (pay) him back. Their debt* will be paid in a year or two. Ted and Cindy and Ralph and Sarah are two very interesting couples.

* twins: *two children born at the same time from the same mother*
* be close to (somebody): *to feel connected with, and to be in a strong relationship with, somebody*
* psychologist: *someone who studies the mind and emotions and their relationship to how people act*
* establish: *to begin something well so that it will last*
* debt: *money that you owe someone*

Present and Past

Read the paragraph about Bob. Write a similar paragraph about yourself or someone who has a problem with where they are living. Use verbs in an appropriate tense.

My friend Bob lives with his family, but he is looking for an apartment. He works at a dental lab* during the day. He takes college classes at night and studies on the weekend, the only free time he has. Bob is having a problem with his younger brothers and sisters, however. They are always making noise or coming into his room when he is trying to study. Last week he didn't finish his school work because they bothered him a lot. He felt angry at them and frustrated because he didn't finish his homework. "Maybe I should get an apartment," Bob thinks. But he isn't thinking of the extra cost and the time that it takes to shop, cook, and clean. I hope he makes the right decision.

Use these questions as a guide:

1. Who do you live with?
2. What problem are you having?
3. Is there a solution to the problem? What?

I live with . . . OR   *My friend Amy lives with . . .*

* dental lab: *a laboratory that makes false teeth*

UNITS
7-8

Present Perfect (*I have done*)

Present Perfect and Past

Put a check (✔) next to the sentence that has the same meaning as the first sentence.

1. This is the first time I've ridden a bicycle.

   _____ a. I've ridden a bicycle before.

   ✔ b. I haven't ridden a bicycle before.

   _____ c. I've ridden a bicycle before, but not for a long time.

2. I just saw your brother downtown.

   _____ a. I saw your brother downtown a little while* ago.

   _____ b. I haven't seen your brother downtown recently.

   _____ c. I've already seen your brother downtown many times.

3. I haven't been to that restaurant for a long time.

   _____ a. I have never been to that restaurant.

   _____ b. This is the first time I've been there.

   _____ c. I ate at that restaurant a long time ago.

4. Paul hasn't eaten anything since last night.

   _____ a. Paul didn't eat anything yesterday.

   _____ b. Paul hasn't eaten anything for two days.

   _____ c. Paul hasn't eaten anything today.

5. My wife has taken three business trips so far this year.

   _____ a. She has left town on business three times this year.

   _____ b. She hasn't traveled for pleasure this year.

   _____ c. She is out of town on business at the moment.

6. The salesman didn't sell any cars yesterday, but he has sold three recently.

   _____ a. He hasn't sold any cars recently.

   _____ b. He's sold three cars in the last few days.

   _____ c. He is selling a car now.

7. Have you ever been to Japan?

   _____ a. Did you go to Japan on your trip to Asia last year?

   _____ b. Have you been to Japan recently?

   _____ c. Have you visited Japan?

8. My father and I never argue now. We get along better than before.

   _____ a. I've never argued with my father.

   _____ b. My father and I have had an argument.

   _____ c. My father and I haven't had an argument recently.

* a little while: *a short time*

EXERCISE 12

Present Perfect (*I have done*)

Complete the conversations. Use the words in parentheses and any other necessary words. Use the present perfect.

1. *A:* (ever / be / to Central America?) *Have you ever been to Central America?*
   B: No, I haven't, but I lived in Venezuela for two years.

2. *A:* We had to wait three hours at the border.
   B: Sorry to hear that. (never / happen / to me) That _____ .

3. *A:* Margaret was a lot friendlier before, wasn't she?
   B: (she / change) Yes, _____ .

4. *A:* (see / Dr. Abbott about your cold yet?) _____
   B: No, I haven't. She's out of town.

5. *A:* What time is your sister going to the bank?
   B: (already / leave) _____

6. *A:* Did your brother like the present that you sent him?
   B: I don't know. (not / get / it yet) He _____ .

7. *A:* (do / anything interesting recently?) _____
   B: Not really. What about you?

8. *A:* (eat / at this restaurant) Is this the first time _____ ?
   B: No, I eat here often.

9. *A:* How is Ben doing these days?
   B: I think he's sick. (not / be) He _____ to work all week.

Present Perfect Continuous (*I have been doing*)

Complete B's answers. Use a phrase from the box in the present perfect continuous.

fix the streets in the area	take aspirin every day	go to a new one	rain here
~~live in our own house~~	wait to see her	~~not sleep well~~	travel a lot on business
take classes at the college	save money		

1. *A:* Do you still live with your wife's parents?

   B: No. We <u>*have been living in our own house*</u> for a year now.

2. *A:* Why are you so tired tonight?

   B: I <u>*haven't been sleeping well*</u> lately.

3. *A:* Are you taking any medication*?

   B: Yes. I _____ for several months.

4. *A:* Your neighborhood wasn't so noisy before. What happened?

   B: They _____ the last two weeks.

5. *A:* I'm impressed with your Chinese. It has really improved.

   B: Thanks. I _____ .

6. *A:* We haven't seen you for a long time. Why not?

   B: I _____ this year.

7. *A:* Do you still shop at the same supermarket?

   B: No. I _____ for several weeks now.

8. *A:* *(on the phone, long distance)* How is your vacation so far?

   B: Terrible. It _____ for three days, and we can't go to the beach.

9. *A:* *(at the doctor's)* Thank you for waiting. The doctor will see you soon.

   B: Finally! I _____ for forty-five minutes!

10. *A:* Do you have enough money to buy a house?

    B: Yes, we _____ since we got married.

   * medication: *medicine like pills, etc.*

Present Perfect Continuous and Present Perfect Simple
(*I have been doing* and *I have done*)

Write a question using the first group of words in parentheses. Use the present perfect continuous or the present perfect simple. Then write an answer using the second group of words.

1. *A:* (how long / you / work / on your car?)

   How long have you been working on your car?

   B: (work / for almost two hours)

   I 've been working for almost two hours .

2. *A:* (how many letters / he / finish?)

   How many letters has he finished?

   B: (write / six letters so far)

   He _____ .

3. *A:* (how long / you / do / your homework?)

   _____

   B: (study / since breakfast)

   I _____ .

4. *A:* (how much money / she / spend / today?)

   _____

   B: (spend / a lot of money)

   _____

5. *A:* (how long / they / dance?)

   _____

   B: (dance / all evening)

   _____

6. *A:* (how many times / you / play / cards / this week?)

   _____

   B: (play / three times)

   I _____ .

7. *A:* (how many rooms / he / paint / today?)

   _____

   B: (finish / three rooms)

   _____

How long have you (been) . . . ?
For and *since*, *When . . . ?* and *How long . . . ?*

**A. Write B's answers. Use the time expression in parentheses with *for, since,* or *ago.*
Use the present perfect (simple or continuous) or the simple past.**

A	B
1. How long have you been using the computer?	(two hours) *I've been using it for two hours.*
2. When did you get your invitation to Jack's wedding?	(a long time) *I got it a long time ago.*
3. How long have you been waiting here?	(a long time) _____
4. How long has your sister been a judge?	(last year) _____
5. When did your brother get married?	(several months) _____
6. How long have you lived here?	(about three years) We _____
7. How long did you live in Cleveland before that?	(a year) We _____
8. How long has it been raining?	(the day before yesterday) _____
9. How long has it been since you bought a new TV?	(1990) I haven't _____

**B. Write questions for the answers. Use the words in parentheses. Use *When* + the
simple past or *How long* + the present perfect.**

A	B
1. (you / move / here?) *When did you move here?*	A month ago.
2. (you / wear / glasses?) *How long have you been wearing glasses?*	Since I was a child.
3. (you / be / sick?) _____	For almost a week now.
4. (you / live / near school?) _____	Since last month.
5. (you / start / your new job?) _____	Two months ago.
6. (your brother / live / in Egypt?) _____	For over a year now.
7. (he / leave / the office?) _____	At 5 o'clock.

NITS
1-13

How long have you (been) . . . ?
For and **since, When . . . ?,** and **How long . . . ?**
Present Perfect and Past (*I have done* and *I did*)

Use your own ideas to complete the sentences in the present perfect (simple or continuous) or simple past.

1. *I have lived* (OR *I have been living . . .*) *in the same house* _____ all my life.
   _____ all my life.

2. *My parents bought a new house* _____ when they got married.
   _____ when they got married.

3. _____ a few months ago.

4. _____ since they got married.

5. _____ for the last two years.

6. _____ since I was born.

7. _____ in 1992.

8. _____ for many years.

9. _____ since I began studying English.

10. _____ all my life.

11. _____ for a long time.

12. _____ many years ago.

13. _____ for a short time.

14. It's been three or four years since _____ .

15. _____ today.

16. _____ last week.

17. _____ this week.

Past Perfect (*I had done*)

Continue the short descriptions with two sentences using the words in parentheses. Use the simple past in one sentence and the past perfect in the other.

1. Ana was very happy when we visited her last night.

   (her son / call / her from Argentina) *Her son had called her from Argentina.*

   (she / tell / us about his job) *She told us about his job.*

2. Someone broke into* the Smiths' house yesterday.

   (they / not be / at home at the time) *They weren't home at the time.*

   (they / leave / a window open) *They had left a window open.*

3. I was walking home from work when I met an old friend.

   (she / be / away for several years) _____

   (we / have / a long talk) _____

4. I was very tired last night.

   (work / very hard at the office) _____

   (not brush / my teeth before going to bed) _____

5. Sam and Amy finally got married.

   (everyone / be / happy for them) _____

   (know / each other for a long time) _____

6. Jim changed a flat tire on his car yesterday.

   (it / be / difficult for him) _____

   (never / do / it before) _____

7. Someone rang the doorbell late last night.

   (Linda / go / to bed early) _____

   (the doorbell / wake / her) _____

   * break into: *to enter a building in order to steal something*

UNIT 15

Past Perfect Continuous (*I had been doing*)

A. Complete the conversations with the words in parentheses. Use the appropriate tense, the past perfect continuous or the past continuous.

1. *A:* Why was Phil angry at us when we met him yesterday?

   B: (wait / a long time) Because *he'd been waiting a long time*   .

2. *A:* Why didn't Sarah see the accident?

   B: (look at / her watch) Because *she was looking at her watch*   .

3. *A:* Why were Roger's eyes so red this morning?

   B: (study / all night) Because _____.

4. *A:* Why didn't Kate want any tea this afternoon?

   B: (drink / coffee all morning) Because _____.

5. *A:* Why was Jennifer so tired at dinner last night?

   B: (jog / in the afternoon) Because _____.

6. *A:* Why didn't Susan go to the movies with you after dinner?

   B: (study / for a test) Because _____.

7. *A:* Why didn't Freddie hear the telephone ring?

   B: (plant / flowers in the garden) Because _____.

8. *A:* Why didn't Tom cook dinner last night?

   B: (cook) Because _____ all day for a party.

B. Rewrite the answers to questions 1 to 5 so that they are complete sentences.

1. *Phil was angry at us when we met him yesterday because he had been waiting a long time.*
2. _____
3. _____
4. _____
5. _____

Have and *have got*

Complete the sentences. Use the word(s) in parentheses and an appropriate form of *have* or *have got*. Some sentences are negative, and some are questions.

1. Julie can't take a long trip this year.

   (a baby) She _had a baby_ _____ last month.

2. Sorry, I can't give you a ride home.

   (a car) I _don't have a car_ OR _haven't got a car_ _____ .

3. I need coins for the telephone.

   (change for a dollar) _Do_ you _have change for a dollar_ _____ ?

    OR _Have_ you _got change for a dollar_ _____ ?

4. I don't feel like going to the movies.

   (a stomachache) I _____ .

5. You're driving to Atlanta?

   (a safe trip) _____ !

6. We couldn't buy many presents.

   (enough money) We _____ .

7. Jason was late to work again this morning.

   (trouble) He _____ finding his keys.

8. *A:* Does Milton go out a lot?

   B: (many friends) No, he _____ .

9. *A:* (fun) _____ the Davidsons _____ on their vacation?
    B: Yes, they said it was great.

10. *A:* What's in the bag?

    B: (some water to drink) I _____ in the bag in case we get thirsty.

11. *A:* My uncle just got out of the hospital.

    B: (an operation) Really? _____ ?

Used to (do)

Read each sentence. Write a new sentence that describes how things were in the past. Use _used to_ or _didn't use to_.

1. There was a gas station on that corner, but it's gone now.

   There used to be a gas station on that corner.

2. The noise from the trains didn't bother us when we moved here, but it has gotten worse.

   The noise from the trains didn't use to bother us.

3. Mark was good looking when he was younger, but he's changed.

   _____

4. I quit smoking ten years ago.

   _____

5. Mr. Simpson was a good father before, but now he yells at his children a lot.

   _____

6. I ate a lot of candy before, but my dentist told me to stop.

   _____

7. My sister worked at that hospital until she got a new job.

   _____

8. Glen and I were good friends, but then something happened.

   _____

9. I get up at five now; I miss sleeping late.

   _____

10. Al and Anne were a happy couple before, but they argue a lot now.

    _____

11. Mrs. Finley has trouble walking now, but she was a good soccer player when she was younger.

    _____

12. We had a beautiful Persian carpet, but we gave it to our daughter.

    _____

13. My neighbors go out to eat all the time now, but they didn't before.

    _____

Present Perfect and Past

Use your own ideas to write new sentences with the underlined words.

1. I <u>have been</u> working at my computer <u>for a long time</u>.

   I have been studying English for a long time.

   My parents have been worried about my brother for a long time.

   My uncle and father have been working at the same place for a long time.

2. I <u>have traveled</u> to Mexico and South America, but I <u>have never been</u> to eastern Europe.

   My parents have traveled all around this country, but they have never been abroad.

   My wife and I have traveled by airplane, but we have never been on a ship.

3. My friends <u>have been</u> married <u>for</u> five years, but they don't have children.

4. My aunt and uncle <u>just</u> bought a new house, but I haven't seen it <u>yet</u>.

5. My brother <u>is very</u> sad these days. He <u>has been that way since</u> he got divorced.

6. <u>I've already</u> read the newspaper, so <u>I don't need to</u> watch the news on TV tonight.

7. I <u>haven't been to</u> the dentist for more than a year.

8. A friend <u>has been</u> exercising for several months, but he <u>hasn't</u> lost much weight.

9. My mother and sister <u>haven't</u> talked to each other <u>since</u> they had an argument.

10. My coworkers and I <u>haven't been</u> working late <u>recently</u>.

11. <u>It's been a long time since</u> I took a vacation.

EXERCISE 22

Present Perfect and Past

Read the passage about a tennis match between two friends. Circle the correct form of the verb.

My friend Paul won our tennis match yesterday because he **1)** had played /(played)/ was playing better than me. Unfortunately, I felt tired half way through the tennis match because I **2)** hadn't eaten / wasn't eating a very good breakfast that morning. An older couple at the park **3)** had been feeding / was feeding the pigeons while they watched us play. The man **4)** wanted / has wanted to give me advice on my tennis game, but his wife **5)** stopped / was stopping / had stopped him from saying anything. I was a little embarrassed when I **6)** realized / have realized that they **7)** watched / were watching / have been watching us play.

Since I **8)** had spent / was spending / had been spending a lot of money on my new tennis racquet, I **9)** had been / was very disappointed in how badly I played yesterday. Paul **10)** was / has been / had been nice about it, though. He **11)** didn't brag*/ hadn't bragged about winning the match. When I **12)** have gotten / got / was getting home after the match, I **13)** had had / had / have had something to eat. **14)** I felt / had felt / have felt much better after I **15)** have eaten / had eaten.

Before we left the tennis courts that morning, Paul and I **16)** have arranged / arranged / were arranging to play tennis again next week. **17)** I have decided / had decided / was deciding that I will practice a lot before our next match and have a good breakfast that day.

  * brag: *to speak with pride, often too proudly, about something you have done*

Present Tenses (*I am doing / I do*) with a Future Meaning

Future

Complete the conversations. Use the words in parentheses. Use the simple present or the present continuous.

1. A: (you / go / anywhere Thursday night?) *Are you going anywhere Thursday night?*

   B: (we / go / to the baseball game) *We're going to the baseball game.* We already have tickets.

2. A: *(at the airport)* (the plane from Chicago / arrive / at 1:15 or 1:50?)

   Does the plane from Chicago arrive at 1:15 or 1:50?

   B: (it / arrive / at 1:25) Actually, _____ .

   (you / meet / someone on the flight?) _____

3. A: I heard you got engaged. (when / you / get married?) _____

   B: Next month. (And we / spend / our honeymoon in Hawaii) _____

4. A: I have to go now. (you / ride / home with me?) _____

   B: No, thanks. I can take the train later. (the last one / run / at midnight) _____

5. A: (you / do / anything tonight?) _____

   B: Yes. (I / do / my grocery shopping) _____ Why?

   A: (Daniel and I / go / to the movies) _____ Would you like to join us?

6. A: (you / pick / me up from school today?) _____

   B: I guess so. What time do you finish on Mondays?

7. A: What time does your brother get off work on Thursdays?

   B: At 4:30, I think. Why?

   A: (I / take / a 7 o'clock flight) _____ , and I need a ride to the airport.

   B: I'm sure he can take you there.

(I'm) going to (do)

A. Use the words in parentheses to write the next sentence. Use _going to_.

1. I've decided to move to a new house.

   (get / a house with a yard) _I'm going to get a house with a yard._

2. How can you talk about taking a vacation when you have no money?

   (where / stay?) _Where are you going to stay?_

3. My parents just bought a new car.

   (take a long trip in it) They _____ sometime soon.

4. Matt drives too fast and doesn't pay attention.

   (have / an accident) He _____ .

5. Amy is marrying a man with no job and little education.

   (be / sorry) She _____ .

6. I am really fed up with my job.

   (quit / soon) _____

7. Adrienne and Todd just bought a new house.

   (have / a party) _____

8. The sinks in the kitchen and bathroom don't work.

   (when / we / fix / them?) _____

B. Read the second half of the sentence. Write the first half, using _was / were going to_ and the words in parentheses.

1. (I / call / you last night) _I was going to call you last night_ , but then I forgot.

2. (my brother / visit / me) _____ , but there were no plane tickets available.

3. (you / help / me last night) _____ , but I guess you forgot.

4. (my parents / take / a trip) _____ , but my father got sick.

5. (sell / my car) _____ , but I decided to keep it.

Present Tenses (*I am doing / I do*) with a Future Meaning (*I'm*) *going to* (*do*)

Circle the most appropriate form of the verb. More than one form may be correct in some sentences.

1. Hurry up! The movie starts in fifteen minutes. We get / are getting /(are going to get) there late.

2. My brother is getting tired of his job. He quits / is quitting / is going to quit when he finds a new one.

3. We have twenty minutes to kill*. According to the sign, the store doesn't open / isn't opening / isn't going to open until 10 A.M. on Mondays.

4. I'm sorry I can't help you move on Saturday. I visit / am visiting / am going to visit my parents this weekend.

5. We usually work until 5 P.M., but we get out / are getting out / are going to get out early today because of the holiday tomorrow.

6. I'd like to go hiking, but I think it rains / is raining / is going to rain this afternoon.

7. Ana needs to be more careful when she cooks. She burns / is burning / is going to burn herself if she isn't careful.

8. I am not going to Los Angeles with my wife next week because I take care of / am taking care of / am going to take care of the children.

9. Don't worry about the kitchen sink. A plumber comes / is coming / is going to come to fix it at 9 A.M. tomorrow morning.

10. Do you have / Are you having / Are you going to have lunch with your friend from college today or tomorrow?

11. I don't give / am not giving / am not going to give you any more money until you pay back the money you borrowed last month.

12. My brother is a teacher, but he doesn't teach / isn't teaching / isn't going to teach next summer if he saves enough money.

* have time to kill: *to have to wait or have extra time (before something happens)*

Will

Write the next sentence. Use the words in parentheses and any other necessary words. Use *will ('ll)*.

1. That suitcase looks too heavy for you.

   (carry / it for you) I _*'ll carry it for you*_ .

2. Thanks for lending me your tools.

   (return / them next week) I _____ .

3. It's cold in here.

   (you / please shut the door?) _____

4. I've been trying to start my computer for half an hour, but something is wrong.

   (not / start) _____

5. The tickets for the concert are very expensive.

   (spend / my extra money on one) I don't think _____ .

6. Why don't you ask Amy for help?

   (explain / the word to you) She _____ .

7. I'm flying to Mexico City next week.

   (need / warm clothes) Do you think I _____ ?

8. I'm sorry I hurt your feelings.

   (not / do / it again) _____

Read the short E-mail from Ted to a friend. Then complete the sentences with *will* ('ll).

From: Ted
Sent: Oct 04, 2003
To: Jim
Subject: marathon

Dear Jim,

We are all excited about the marathon here next Saturday. Fortunately, the weather
has been nice all week, and it doesn't rain much this time of year.

Alice and Ben are both running in the race. Alice is a good athlete and has trained*
a lot. She's has a good chance of doing well in the race. But Ben is pretty lazy and
hasn't trained at all. In my opinion, he doesn't even have a good chance of finishing
the race.

There are many good runners in the race, so no one can predict the winner. But the
race should be interesting to watch. I plan to get there early so I can get a good place
to stand.

I hope to hear from you soon.

Best wishes,
Ted

1. (the weather / be / nice on Saturday) Ted thinks *the weather will be nice on Saturday* .

2. (be / a good race) He thinks it _____ .

3. (finish / the race) He doubts Ben _____ .

4. (do well in the race) He thinks Alice _____ .

5. (who / win the race) He isn't sure _____ .

6. (probably get a good place to stand) Ted plans to go to the race early, so _____

_____ .

* train: *to prepare by exercising and practicing*

EXERCISE 28

I will and *I'm going to*

Complete the sentences. Use the verb in parentheses and *will* or *going to*.

1. We _are going to buy_ (buy) a new car next September when we return from abroad.

2. *A:* Amy lost her job.

   B: Really? She _won't have_ (not / have) any trouble finding another one.

3. *A:* I see that there is a For Sale sign in front of your house.

   B: Now that all our children are away in college, my wife and I _____ _____ (move) to a smaller house.

4. *(on the phone)* Why didn't you tell me you were in the hospital? I _____ _____ (come) and see you right away.

5. Mike eats a lot of sweets and never brushes his teeth. _____ (lose) them.

6. I _____ (stop) at the supermarket for some shampoo while I'm out. Do you need anything?

7. *A:* It's Uncle John's birthday next week.

   B: Is it? I _____ (buy) a card to send him.

8. Sam and Sheila _____ (have) a party to celebrate their wedding anniversary next Saturday.

9. I'm sorry I forgot your birthday. I _____ (make) dinner for you sometime this week.

10. *A:* We need tickets for our trip.

    B: I know. That's why I _____ (go) to the travel agent tomorrow morning.

11. Mike and Amy have changed their minds*. _____ (not / get) married after all*.

   * change (one's) mind: *to change your decision or opinion*
   * after all: *in spite of what was decided before; in the end*

Read about Debbie's day. Then, on the next page, put a check by statements that are true about Debbie's day tomorrow. More than one statement in each group may be true.

Debbie's routine* doesn't change much from day to day. Debbie and her husband, Greg, get up at 7 A.M. and take showers. At 7:30, Debbie gives her baby a bath while Greg makes breakfast. Greg and Debbie eat together at 8 before he leaves for work at 8:15. After he leaves, Debbie feeds the baby, and that takes about a half hour. Then she does the breakfast dishes while her baby plays. At 9, while the baby is taking a nap*, Debbie does housework. At 10, she takes her baby for a walk until 11. Debbie watches a TV program from 11 to 11:30 while the baby plays on the floor. Then she cooks lunch. She and her baby have lunch from 12 to 12:30.

* routine: *usual way of doing things*
* take a nap: *to sleep for a short time during the day*

EXERCISE CONTINUES ▶ ▶

1. At 7:10

_____ a. Debbie will be sleeping.

✔ b. Debbie will be taking a shower.

_____ c. Greg will be in bed.

✔ d. Debbie will already have gotten up.

2. At 7:45

_____ a. Greg will be making breakfast.

_____ b. Debbie will be giving her baby a bath.

_____ c. Debbie will be eating breakfast with her husband.

_____ d. Debbie will have eaten breakfast.

3. At 8:30

_____ a. Debbie will be feeding her baby.

_____ b. Greg will be leaving for work.

_____ c. Greg will have left for work.

_____ d. Debbie will have had breakfast.

4. At 9:15

_____ a. The baby will take a nap.

_____ b. Debbie will be cleaning the house.

_____ c. Debbie will have finished her housework.

_____ d. The baby will be sleeping.

5. At 10:30

_____ a. Greg will be at work.

_____ b. Debbie and the baby won't be at home.

_____ c. Debbie and the baby will have returned from their walk.

_____ d. Debbie and the baby will be taking a walk.

6. At 11:15

_____ a. Debbie will be watching TV.

_____ b. The baby will be taking a nap.

_____ c. Debbie and the baby will have returned from their walk.

_____ d. Debbie will be cooking lunch.

When I do / When I've done   When and *if*

Complete the sentences with one of the following verbs. Use a verb from the box in the simple present or in the future with *will*. Some sentences are negative.

bother	call	decide	~~feel~~	feel	find out*	get	go
move	paint	~~promise~~	~~rain~~	reach	regret	stop	

1. You __*will feel*__ better when you've had something to eat.

2. My brother will lend my sister the money she needs if she __*promises*__ to pay him back in a month.

3. If there are no clouds in the sky tonight, it probably __*won't rain*__ tomorrow morning.

4. Can I stay at your place until the rain _____ ?

5. Could you please get me some envelopes when you _____ to the store?

6. Kim _____ me when she's finished with the report.

7. Mark will tell us the results of his lab tests* as soon as he _____ about them.

8. I won't buy new clothes if I _____ the job I applied for.

9. *(on an airplane)* Please stay in your seats until the plane _____ the terminal.

10. They _____ the outside of the house until the weather is drier.

11. Where will your sister live when she _____ to Seattle?

12. Let me know as soon as you _____ which movie you're going to.

13. I don't think you _____ it if you buy that book. It's wonderful.

14. You _____ much better after you've had a good night's sleep.

15. That bee _____ you if you don't move.

   * find out: *to learn something, usually by asking or searching for the information*
   * lab tests: *medical tests or analyses (of blood, etc.)*

Read the paragraph. Write a similar paragraph about yourself, a family member, or a friend. Write about your plans for the coming week. Use appropriate verb forms to express the future.

The weather will probably be nice this week. That's good because I am going to paint the outside of my house. A friend is going to help me, and we'll probably need three or four days to finish. My friend is flying here from Miami, and he arrives tomorrow. I'm picking him up at the airport at 10:30 in the morning. Then we're going to decide on the colors and buy the paint. I don't think it will rain. If it rains, I will just show my friend around* Atlanta. We'll have a real vacation instead of a working vacation!

Use these questions as a guide:

1. What are you going to do next week?
2. How do you think the weather will be?
3. Will the weather affect your plans?
4. Is anyone visiting you next week?
5. What are you going to do together?

_____

_____

_____

_____

_____

_____

_____

_____

_____

_____

_____

_____

_____

* show someone around (somewhere): *to show someone the sights and attractions of a place*

Modals

Write the second sentence. Use *can('t)* or *could(n't)* + a phrase from the box. Add any other necessary words.

hear airplanes all night	go out for a week	~~understand everything~~
do anything to help	~~come to your party~~	find my wallet
speak	play several musical instruments	see the screen* very well

1. Thanks for the invitation. Unfortunately, we _can't come to your party_
   next weekend.

2. When I lived in Brazil, my Portuguese was really good. _I could understand everything._

3. Poor David just broke his leg. He _____ .

4. *A:* Did you pay the electrician?
   B: No, _____ .

5. *(in a movie theater)* Can we change seats? I _____ .

6. The hotel near the airport was noisy. I _____ .

7. Sheryl is very talented. She _____ .

8. I'm sure you'll enjoy your trip to North Africa. _____
   any French?

9. We felt terrible when we saw the accident. We _____ .

* screen: *the flat, white surface where a movie is shown*

EXERCISE 33

Can, could, and (be) able to

Complete the sentences using *could* or *was/were able to*. Some answers are negative, and more than one answer is correct in some sentences.

1. Kevin looked for a part-time job for a month, and finally he _was able to_ get a job in a restaurant after school.

2. Because I had to baby-sit, I _couldn't_ OR _wasn't able to_ go to the concert in the park last Tuesday night.

3. Peter hadn't left for the airport when his friends called, so they _____ let him know that their flight was late.

4. The store on the corner usually has a lot of bread, but when I went there yesterday, I _____ get any because the delivery truck hadn't come.

5. Javier can speak several languages well. He _____ speak English fairly well even before he started to take English classes, and now his English is even better.

6. Jessica worked at two part-time jobs last year, so she _____ buy an inexpensive used car a few months ago.

7. The company developed a good product, and it _____ persuade many stores to sell it, so the company is now growing rapidly.

8. I _____ swim all the way out to the boat in the harbor, so my friends swam there without me.

9. It was raining yesterday, so we _____ work in the garden.

10. Because the family left the city early Friday morning, they _____ avoid the traffic, and they arrived at the beach in less than an hour.

Can, could, and *(be) able to*
Could (do) and *could have (done)*

Circle the correct form of the verb.

1. My sister (could have bought)/ could buy / was able to buy an American car, but she bought a Japanese car instead.

2. When I finished shopping, I could find / was able to find my car in the parking lot right away, but I couldn't have found / couldn't find my car keys.

3. Lucia can't speak / couldn't speak / couldn't have spoken English very well last year, but she can have / could have / could have had long conversations in English now.

4. The couple in the restaurant were arguing so loudly that I could have heard / could hear everything they said to each other.

5. Please give the tickets back to me if you weren't able to go / can't go / manage to go to the concert tonight.

6. Jason isn't at work today. It could mean / could have meant he's having trouble with his asthma* again.

7. Amy couldn't find / can't find / hasn't been able to find a good apartment since she moved here.

8. I could get / was able to get / manage to get an appointment with the dentist today after I explained that I had a bad toothache.

9. We could stay / could have stayed / were able to stay at the party a lot longer, but my wife and I were both tired, so we went home at 9:30.

10. Most of the flights were sold out*, but Julie was finally able to get / could finally get plane tickets for next Sunday.

11. The word "light" could be / can be a noun, an adjective, or a verb.

12. I ordered chicken soup, but I couldn't taste / couldn't have tasted any chicken in it.

13. My boss spoke so quickly on the phone that I couldn't understand / couldn't have understood what he wanted.

* asthma: *an illness that causes difficult breathing*
* sold out: *completely sold; for example, no tickets are left*

Must (*You must be tired*, etc.)

Read the situation. Use the words in parentheses to write a sentence with *must* or *must not* in an appropriate tense.

1. Paul hasn't played tennis for ages.

   (have / trouble with his back) *He must be having trouble with his back.*

2. Jerry knows everything about the stars and planets.

   (study / astronomy in school) *He must have studied astronomy in school.*

3. Your boss and his wife never mention anything about children.

   (have / children) *They must not have children.*

4. The Carvers' car is never outside their house on Sunday mornings.

   (go / to church) They _____.

5. Jack and Alice always invite me to dinner on Sundays when they're in town. I haven't heard from them this week.

   (be / here) _____

6. Sam's taken the bus to work every day this week.

   (run / well these days) His car _____.

7. Sheila was married when I met her, but she tells people she's single now.

   (get / divorced) _____

8. Joe is usually in such a good mood*, but he's been in a terrible mood* lately.

   (bother / him) Something _____.

9. They gave everyone at work new dictionaries last Friday, but Paul doesn't have one.

   (be / at work last Friday) Paul _____.

10. On his way home, Al turned left instead of right on his street.

    (think / about something else) _____

    * be in a good mood: *to be happy, friendly, content*
    * be in a terrible mood: *to be unhappy, unfriendly, discontent*

Circle the correct form.

1. *A:* Why isn't Joanne here?

   B: I don't know. She (may have gotten)/ may get stuck* in traffic.

2. *A:* Are your parents flying to Montreal next week?

   B: They haven't decided. They may drive / may as well drive instead.

3. *A:* I wonder why Kim isn't at home.

   B: She may go / may have gone to her mother's.

4. *A:* *(at the door)* Why doesn't Julia answer the doorbell?

   B: She might be taking / might take a nap*.

5. *A:* *(in an office)* Does anyone know where George is?

   B: He might go / might have gone out to lunch.

6. *A:* Who do you suppose broke this dish?

   B: It couldn't have been / might not have been / couldn't be my little brother.
   He hasn't been home all day.

7. *A:* Do you have any idea why Mark hasn't called us?

   B: No, I don't. He might have left / might have been leaving town.

8. *A:* Why don't Sally and her brother speak to each other anymore?

   B: I'm not sure. They may have / may have had / may have been having an argument
   or something.

9. *A:* Did Kevin take his family to Houston for the weekend?

   B: I saw his children here on Saturday, so he might not have taken / couldn't have taken
   them to Houston.

10. *A:* Why are there so many cars in front of the Baxters' house?

    B: I don't know. They might have / might be having a party.

* stuck (past participle of *stick*): *not able to move*
* take a nap: *to sleep for a short time during the day*

May and *might*

A. Rewrite the sentences. Use *may* or *might* in place of *maybe* and *perhaps*.

1. Perhaps I'll take a few weeks off at Christmas.

   I might take a few days off at Christmas. OR *I may take . . .*

2. Maybe your sister isn't coming to the party.

   Your sister may not be coming to the party. OR *Your sister might not be coming . . .*

3. Perhaps George was in a bad mood yesterday.

   George might have been in a bad mood yesterday. OR *George may have been . . .*

4. Maybe the post office doesn't deliver mail on the Presidents' Day holiday.

   _____

5. Maybe your son is trying to call you right now.

   _____

6. Maybe Tom forgot to call his grandparents.

   _____

7. Perhaps the Hennigans sold their car to buy something else.

   _____

8. Perhaps Carol wasn't kidding when she said she was sick.

   _____

B. Rewrite the sentences. Use *might be able to* or *might have to*.

1. Maybe you can wear your brother's suit to the wedding.

   You might be able to wear your brother's suit to the wedding.

2. Maybe I'll have to work this weekend.

   _____

3. Maybe I can help you Saturday if I don't have to work.

   _____

4. Perhaps you won't have to give me a ride after all.

   _____

Answer each question with two suggestions. Use *may* or *might* in an appropriate form and the words in parentheses.

1. *A:* Why is Sam looking at the floor?

   B: 1. (look / for his contact lens) *He might be looking for his contact lens.*

   2. (drop / his contact lens) *He may have dropped his contact lens.*

2. *A:* I can't find my notebook. Have you seen it?

   B: 1. (be / on the bookshelf) It *might be on the bookshelf* .

   2. (forget / it at school) You _____ .

3. *A:* Why does Sarah look so sad today?

   B: 1. (miss / her boyfriend) She _____ .

   2. (have / an argument with her father) _____

4. *A:* Why is Reggie eating so little tonight?

   B: 1. (be / worried about something) He _____ .

   2. (eat / a lot for lunch) _____

5. *A:* Isn't Rose coming to the party? She's usually so punctual*, but she's not here yet.

   B: 1. (do / something else tonight) She _____ .

   2. (forget / about the party) _____

6. *A:* Why is Bob taking the bus to work these days?

   B: 1. (be / at the mechanic's) His car _____ .

   2. (sell / his car) He _____ .

7. *A:* I wonder how Angela's accident happened.

   B: 1. (not / see / the other car) She _____ .

   2. (think / of something else) _____

* punctual: *on time*

EXERCISE 39

Have to and *must*

Circle the correct form.

1. I have got to / (had to) / must work late last night.

2. Jim said, "Sorry. I can't stay any longer. I <u>have got to / had to</u> leave the party early to pick someone up at the airport in half an hour."

3. All of us <u>must / had to</u> try to help people who are poorer than we are.

4. I <u>mustn't / don't have to</u> work next Saturday, so I can go to the country with you.

5. Passengers on an airplane <u>haven't got to / must not / don't have to</u> leave their seats during takeoff and landing.

6. People <u>don't have to / must not</u> take the host or hostess* a present when they are invited to dinner, but it's a nice gesture*.

7. My father said I <u>don't have to / must not</u> use his new car under any circumstances*.

8. Paul <u>had to / must / has got to</u> go to Tokyo on business last week.

9. You <u>have got to / had to</u> help me. No one else will.

10. Ben <u>had to / must</u> take his wife to the hospital in the middle of the night because of an emergency. She had a pain in her stomach.

11. We <u>had to / have got to</u> get up early to catch a 6 o'clock flight tomorrow morning.

12. The students <u>don't have to / mustn't</u> buy new books for the course. They can use their old ones.

   * host/hostess: *a man/woman who receives others in his or her home as guests*
   * nice gesture: *a nice action; a nice thing to do*
   * not under any circumstances: *in no case; never*

Have to and *must*

Complete the conversations. Use the words in parentheses, including an appropriate form of *have to*.

1. *A:* Why are you so serious? Is something wrong?

   B: (I / have / make / an important decision) No, *I have to make an important decision* .

2. *A:* (we / have / get up early tomorrow?) *Do we have to get up early tomorrow?*
   B: No, we can sleep until 10 A.M.

3. *A:* Do you get off work at 5 P.M. every day?

   B: (I / have / work / late last night) Usually, but _____ .

4. *A:* Can you and your wife come to dinner tomorrow night?

   B: (my wife / have / go to a meeting) I can, but _____ .

5. *(on the phone) A:* Is your brother there?

   B: (he / have / go back / to work) No, _____ .

6. *A:* Did the tire store fix your flat tire?

   B: (I / not / have / pay / anything) Yes, and _____ .
   The repair was free.

7. *A:* There's a public phone. Don't you want to make a phone call?

   B: (I / have / call / my travel agent about my plane tickets) Yes, _____

   _____ .

8. *A:* (you / have / go / to the hospital last night?) _____
   B: No, I wasn't that sick.

9. *A:* When does Barb need her book back?

   B: (we / not / have / return / it) _____ She gave it
   to us as a gift.

10. *A:* (you have / have / a driver's license to drive in your country?) _____

    _____

    B: Yes, it's the law.

Should

Complete the sentences with *should (have)* + the verb in parentheses in the correct form. Some sentences are negative.

1. If you're unhappy with your present job, I think you *should look* (look) for another one tomorrow.

2. Aren't you cold in just a shirt? You *should be wearing* (wear) a sweater in weather like this.

3. Jerry spoke angrily to his boss and lost his job. Jerry *shouldn't have lost* (lose) his temper*.

4. You've known all week that we were driving to the city today. You _____ _____ (buy) gas before.

5. The bad weather will slow us down, but we _____ (get) there before dark.

6. Ted's in the cafeteria drinking coffee again. He _____ _____ (work) . He _____ (take) a break.

7. Andrew has exams tomorrow, but I saw him out dancing last night. He _____ _____ (study) for his exams.

8. I am really worried about the children. They _____ (be) here an hour ago.

9. It's a popular movie, but we _____ (have) much trouble getting tickets on a Monday afternoon. Let's go.

10. The boss got angry at Ben because he was talking on his cell phone during the meeting. Ben _____ (talk) on his cell phone then.

11. This book is overdue*. You _____ (return) it last week.

12. I know you're upset, but don't you think you _____ (think) about it a little more before quitting your job?

* lose (one's) temper: *not to be able to control your anger*
* overdue: *not returned on time*

UNIT
32

Subjunctive (*I suggest you do*)

Jerry broke his leg and will be wearing a cast* for a while. Read the advice he got from various people. Then write what each person suggested or recommended he do.

His teacher: "Use this time to catch up on* your reading."

The nurse: "Don't walk without crutches*."

His father: "Put a pillow under your leg to be more comfortable."

His mother: "You should drink a lot of milk to help your bones heal*."

His friend from school: "Call me every day to get the homework."

His brother: "Take aspirin if your leg hurts a lot."

The doctor: "Don't walk on your leg for a few days."

1. His teacher suggested <u>*he use the time to catch up on his reading*</u>   .

2. The nurse recommended <u>*he not walk without crutches*</u>   .

3. His father suggested _____ .

4. His mother recommended _____ .

5. His friend suggested _____ .

6. His brother recommended _____ .

7. The doctor recommended _____ .

* cast: *plaster (usually) used to hold broken bones in place*
* catch up (on something): *to spend time on something that you need to do but haven't been able to earlier*
* crutches: *special sticks with a piece that fits under the arm for support while walking*
* heal: *to get better*

Had better   *It's time . . .*

Read the situations. Write sentences with *had better* or *had better not* + the words in parentheses.

1. Mary has gotten to work late three times this week, and she might lose her job.

   (get to work late again) She *had better not get to work late again* .

2. Tim has had a toothache for a while, and he may lose his tooth if he doesn't see a dentist.

   (see a dentist soon) He _____ .

3. Bob typed a business letter, but it's full of spelling mistakes. The company will think he's not very careful.

   (send the letter that way) He _____ .

4. Lisa has enough food for five people, but she invited eight people to dinner. There's going to be a problem.

   (get more food) She _____ .

5. Joe promised to take his children to the movies, but now he's tired and doesn't want to go. The children will be very disappointed if they don't go.

   (break his promise) He _____ .

6. You and your friend want to play tennis, but the tennis court is wet from rain. You might fall down.

   (play later) We _____ .

7. You haven't seen your aunt for a long time, and she's sick.

   (call my aunt today) I _____ .

8. You and a friend are on a trip, but there's not much gas in the car. You will run out of gas soon.

   (stop and buy some gas) We _____ .

Had better   It's time . . .

A. Complete the sentences. Use *had better* where possible. Otherwise, use *should*.

1. You <u>*had better*</u> be careful. That ladder you are on looks like it might fall.

2. Sandra and Ted often leave their door unlocked. They <u>*should*</u> be more careful.

3. The children _____ be in bed when we get home, or they'll be sorry.

4. Most American parents think children _____ have a regular bed time, especially on school nights.

5. We _____ invite George to the party, or his feelings will be hurt.

6. We _____ get to the box office early, or we won't get tickets to the concert.

7. I think no one under the age of eighteen _____ drive.

8. Don't you think people _____ use their cars less to reduce pollution and stop the damage to the environment?

B. Rewrite the sentences. Use *It's time.*

1. Amy has had a cold for weeks. I think she should see a doctor very soon.
   <u>*It's time Amy saw a*</u>_____ doctor.

2. Our TV is fifteen years old. We should buy a new one.
   It's time we _____ a new TV.

3. We really need to do something about homeless people in this country.
   _____

4. It's getting late. Let's go home.
   _____ home.

5. You're an adult now. You should be more responsible.
   _____ responsible.

6. It's almost 7:30. We should have had dinner before now.
   _____ dinner.

Can / Could / Would you . . . ?, etc.   (Requests, Offers, Permission, and Invitations)

Complete the conversations with *can*, *could*, *would*, or *may* and any other necessary words.

1. A: _Would you like to go_____ to the wedding of a friend of mine?
   B: Sure. When is it?

2. You: _Can / OR Could / OR May /_____ have a menu, please?
   Waiter: Yes, one moment, please.

3. A: Do you think I _____ borrow your bike?
   B: Sure, but I need it an hour from now.

4. A: _____ a glass of water?
   B: Yes, please. I'm very thirsty.

5. A: _____ hang up your coat?
   B: Oh, thanks. That's nice of you.

6. A: _____ you close the door, please?
   B: Sure. Sorry I left it open.

7. A: _____ a piece of fruit?
   B: Yes, thank you.

8. A: _____ get you something to read?
   B: Thank you. I'd like that.

9. A: Do you think _____ give me a ride to work?
   B: Of course. What time do you want to leave?

10. A: Do you think _____ leave the meeting early tomorrow?
    B: Yes, you already know what we're going to discuss.

11. A: _____ have change for ten dollars?
    B: Let me see if I have it.

12. A: Do you think _____ talk a little more loudly?
    B: Of course. Sorry.

13. A: _____ go out to eat?
    B: Yes, I really would. Where shall we go?

Complete the sentences about yourself and others.

1. When I was ten, I could *play baseball pretty well and ice-skate*   .
   When I was ten, I could *speak three languages*   .
   When I was ten, _____ .

2. I was very tired last night, but I was still able to *read the paper before going to bed* .
   I was very tired last night, but I was still able to *cook dinner for myself*   .
   I was very tired last night, but I was still able to _____ .

3. When people don't return your phone calls, they might _____ .

4. When driving a car, you should _____ .

5. I'm lucky that _____ helped me with my problem.
   I couldn't have _____ .

6. My plans are uncertain. I may _____ .

7. I sometimes can't go out with friends because I have to _____ .

8. You need more exercise. You should _____ .

9. My friends and I have a problem with _____ .
   No one was able to _____ .

10. The travel agent recommended that I _____ .

11. The cake cost a lot of money. You should have _____ .

12. It's time that we _____ .

13. My friend wasn't at the corner at noon, so he must have _____ .

14. All drivers must _____ .

15. I am gaining weight, and my doctor suggested that I _____ .

Use your own ideas to write new sentences with the underlined words.

1. My friends in Australia <u>must</u> be very busy <u>because</u> I haven't heard from them in ages.

   My friend Josh must have a lot to do because he hasn't called me for a long time.
   Everyone must know who Mohandas Gandhi was because he was so important.

2. <u>This city should</u> build more parks for people to use.

   This city should be cleaner. People should take better care of it.
   This city should make jobs for people. There are many unemployed people here.

3. My friend Sarah <u>must not</u> make very much money. She's very careful about how much she spends when we go out.

   _____ .

4. I'm good at remembering things, so I <u>don't have to</u> make lists or write things down.

   _____ .

5. When I visited my friend, he was watching TV. He <u>should have been</u> studying for his exam.

   _____ .

6. My uncle <u>might not have</u> felt well last night – he was unusually quiet all evening.

   _____ .

7. My brother <u>has to</u> work this weekend, so I <u>may not be able</u> to see him.

   _____ .

8. I'm not happy with my job. <u>It's time</u> I looked for a different one.

   _____ .

9. My parents <u>didn't insist that</u> I go to college, but they <u>recommended</u> I continue my education after high school.

   _____ .

UNITS
35-36

If I do . . . and *If I did . . .*
If I knew . . . I wish I knew . . .

Conditionals and "Wish"

Read the paragraph about a bad boss. Complete the *if*-sentences using the information in the paragraph.

Frank is not a very popular boss because he doesn't respect us. He is not honest, so we don't trust him. He isn't efficient because he's so disorganized. Most people don't work hard because he gives raises to people he likes, not to people who work hard. He doesn't answer questions clearly, so we don't understand him. He has a lot of meetings that last past working hours, so we can't go home on time. He gets angry for no reason, so everyone is afraid of him. He confuses us because he changes his mind a lot. We are not happy because he isn't a good boss. In fact, he is a terrible boss.

1. He would be more popular *if he respected us* .

2. If he were more honest, *we would trust him* .

3. If he weren't so disorganized, _____ .

4. If he gave raises fairly, _____ .

5. We would understand him _____ .

6. If he didn't have a lot of late meetings, _____ .

7. We wouldn't be afraid _____ .

8. He wouldn't confuse us _____ .

9. We'd be happy _____ .

If I knew . . .   I wish I knew . . .

**Use the words in parentheses to write what each person wishes for now.
Put the verb in the correct form. Some sentences are negative.**

1. (have / a broken leg)
   Kerry wishes *she didn't have a broken leg*   .

2. (have / a car)
   Alfred wishes *he had a car*   .

3. (work / in an office)
   Mike wishes _____.

4. (rain / outside right now)
   I wish it _____.

5. (can / afford / a new car)
   Kevin and Sue _____.

EXERCISE CONTINUES ▶ ▶

6. (live / near the ocean)

Brandon _____ .

7. (be / married)

Sylvia _____ .

8. (have / thirteen cats)

Mary Jo _____ .

9. (have to / get up / so early)

Julio and Marta _____ .

NIT
37

If I had known . . .   I wish I had known . . .

Look at the pictures and the explanations in the box to find the answers to the questions. Write an answer with *if*.

✔He didn't have enough money. She was outside the classroom.   They weren't at home. He wasn't able to find his dictionary.   It was a stormy day. She was on her bike.   ✔He put too much salt in it. He didn't feel well.

1. *A:* Why didn't Frank go to Hawaii?

   B: _If he had had enough money, he would have_
   gone to Hawaii.

2. *A:* Why didn't his family eat Joe's soup?

   B: _If he hadn't put too much salt in it, his family_
   would have eaten it.

3. *A:* Why didn't the tourists go swimming yesterday?

   B: _____

   _____

EXERCISE CONTINUES ▶ ▶

Conditionals and "Wish" Units 35–38   **53**

4. *A:* Why didn't Regina hear the teacher's announcement?

   B: _____

   _____

5. *A:* Why didn't Sid eat breakfast?

   B: _____

   _____

6. *A:* Why didn't the Smiths receive the package yesterday?

   B: _____

   _____

7. *A:* Why didn't Jessica stop to buy groceries yesterday?

   B: _____

   _____

8. *A:* Why didn't Bob look up the new word in the
   dictionary?

   B: _____

   _____

If I had known . . .   I wish I had known . . .

Write sentences with *I wish* + the words in parentheses. Some sentences should be negative.

1. I'm starving*.

   (eat breakfast this morning) *I wish I had eaten breakfast this morning.*

2. Maria is angry at me.

   (tell other people her secret) *I wish I hadn't told other people her secret.*

3. We turned down* the Lees's invitation.

   (accept it) I wish we _____ .

4. Your comment hurt my feelings.

   (be more considerate*) I wish you _____ .

5. I didn't know you were in the hospital last week.

   (tell me) I wish someone _____ .

6. That's a wonderful idea!

   (think of it) I wish I _____ .

7. I can't go away for a vacation this year.

   (spend so much money on my car) _____ .

8. It's raining now.

   (bring my umbrella this morning) _____ .

9. I'm not sure Jack is very experienced.

   (listen to his advice) _____ .

10. Ted decided to change jobs very quickly.

    (have more time to think about it) He wishes _____ .

11. My cousin got married in another country, but I didn't have enough money to go.

    (be able to go) _____ .

* be starving: *to be very, very hungry*
* turn down: *to refuse*
* considerate: *kind and caring about others*

EXERCISE 52

Would   I wish . . . would

Ted and Jerry are brothers. They share a bedroom, but they don't get along very well. Each one wishes the other were different. Read what they say about each other. Then write what each wishes. Use the words in parentheses and *would* or *wouldn't*.

Ted   Jerry

Ted:
Jerry never asks me for things that he wants to borrow. He just takes them. He never makes his bed, and he leaves his clothes on the floor. And he stays up late to talk on the telephone, so I can't sleep. Our mom gets angry about our messy* room, but it's not my fault!

Jerry:
Ted is so bossy*. He tells me to make my bed. He blames me for the mess in our room. He acts like a father, more than like a brother. And he goes to bed so early! I can't do anything in our room at night. He's impossible!

Ted:

1. (borrow) *I wish Jerry would ask me for things that he wants to borrow.*

2. (bed) I wish he would _____ .

3. (clothes) I wish Jerry _____ .

4. (stay up late) I wish he _____ .

5. (messy room) I wish Mom wouldn't _____ .

Jerry:

6. (bossy) I wish Ted _____ .

7. (my bed) I wish he _____ .

8. (mess) _____

9. (a father) _____

10. (to bed so early) _____

* messy: *dirty, disorderly*
* bossy: *fond of telling people what to do*

Conditionals and "Wish"

Use your own ideas to write new sentences with the underlined words.

1. <u>If I</u> was offered a job in Australia, <u>I would</u> take it.

   If I had a car, I would learn to drive.

   If I had more money, I would give some to my parents.

   If I wasn't tired, I would go out tonight.

   _____ .

2. <u>I wish there</u> were more to do in this town.

   I wish there were fewer people on the beach.

   I wish there weren't so many grammar rules in English!

   _____ .

3. My family <u>wishes I would</u> get married and have children.

   _____

4. <u>I could</u> get a bigger place to live <u>if</u> I had more money.

   _____

5. <u>I wouldn't have</u> called my friend last night <u>if I had</u> known he was sleeping.

   _____

6. <u>I wish I had</u> remembered to call my parents on their anniversary.

   _____

7. <u>If I had</u> known the traffic police officer was hiding behind the bush, <u>I would have</u> driven more slowly.

   _____

8. My younger brother <u>would always</u> ask me to drive him places when I first got my driver's license.

   _____

9. <u>I wish I hadn't</u> stayed up so late last night.

   _____

Complete the sentences with the words in parentheses. Use passive verbs in the simple present or the simple past.

1. You have to pay extra for the batteries. (they / not include) *They aren't included* in the price of the flashlight.

2. (Mrs. Chen's dog / kill) _____ in an accident. She is very sad.

3. (elections / hold) How often _____ in the United States?

4. (Mary / fire) _____ for missing work too often.

5. (flights / sometimes cancel) _____ when the weather is bad.

6. (I / accuse) _____ of exaggerating the facts of the story, but I swear* I told exactly what happened.

7. (your sweater / make) Where _____ ? It's very nice.

8. (not / know / by many people) The new vice president _____ right now, but he will be.

9. (the accident / cause) The police said _____ by the fact that the driver was drinking.

10. (the first rocket / send) _____ into space by the Americans or the Russians?

11. (this letter / not / pronounce) _____ the same in Spanish and English, so be careful.

12. (his shoes / cover / with mud) _____ , so his wife told him to take them off when he came in the house.

13. (many houses / damage) _____ by floods* every year.

* swear: *to promise very seriously to tell the truth*
* flood: *water covering a large area of land that is usually dry*

Passive (*is done / was done*)
Passive (*be / been / being done*)

Complete B's answers. Use a passive verb in an appropriate form and the words in parentheses. Some answers are negative.

A	B
1. Do they grow coffee in Chile?	(in Brazil and Colombia) No. Coffee *is grown* *in Brazil and Colombia* .
2. Did you paint your garage?	(by our handyman*) No. It was _____ .
3. I can pay the bills next week, right?	(immediately) No. They should _____ .
4. Are you using the computer right now?	(by someone else) I'm not, but it _____ .
5. Have you cleaned the fridge recently?	(for weeks) No. It _____ .
6. Are they going to build the new highway this year?	(next year) No. It _____ .
7. Do they make polyester from cotton?	(from oil) No. Polyester _____ .
8. Did the police find any evidence* at the scene of the crime*?	(nearby) No. But some evidence _____ .
9. Should I wash your new sweater?	(dry-clean) No. My new sweater has to _____ .
10. Were you using the telephone a few minutes ago?	(by my secretary) No, but it _____ .
11. Did anyone call the police after the accident last night?	(immediately) No. The police should _____ , but they weren't.
12. Did anyone deliver a package for me today?	(deliver) I don't know. A package might _____ .

* handyman: *a person who fixes things in other people's houses for pay*
* evidence: *something that provides information about a crime*
* scene of the crime: *the place where a crime happened*

UNITS
39-40
Passive (*is done / was done*)
Passive (*be / been / being done*)

Read the passage about Tony's job. Then complete the passage using the verbs in parentheses in the appropriate active or passive form.

My friend Tony has had a lot of problems in his job at a telephone company. He

1) _was hired_ (hire) two months ago, and everything 2) _started_ (start) out

perfectly. He 3) _____ (work) very hard in the beginning because he wanted to please

his boss. Tony 4) _____ (offer) to work overtime, and his offer 5) _____

(accept). He 6) _____ (come) to work early and 7) _____ (leave) late.

However, he 8) _____ (not pay) for the extra work. He 9) _____

(complain) to his boss, but nothing 10) _____ (do) about the problem. Tony recently

11) _____ (ask) for a day off, but his request 12) _____ (refuse).

Therefore, he had to 13) _____ (miss) his brother's high school graduation.

The company also 14) _____ (promise) to pay for computer classes, so Tony took a

class at the college. However, when Tony asked to 15) _____ (reimburse*) for the

class, his boss told him that the company was not paying for classes anymore.

It is clear to Tony that he will never 16) _____ (promote) in the company. He now

wants to 17) _____ (quit) his job, but he does not want to 18) _____

(give) a bad recommendation when he leaves. Also, he knows it will not look good if he

19) _____ (leave) a job he has had for only a few months. Tony has a real problem:

he feels he has to stay at a job that he does not like.

* reimburse: *to pay back money to somebody*

N I T
42

It is said that . . .   He is said to . . .   (be) supposed to . . .

Choose the sentence on the right that most logically follows the sentence on the left. Write the letter in the blank.

_h_ 1. What are you doing at home?

     2. You shouldn't take that medicine until lunch time.

     3. I'd like to see that Brazilian film we read about.

     4. We've had rain for three days in a row.

     5. How could you vote for a candidate* like her?

     6. They're still looking for the lost hiker.

     7. Why don't you make an appointment with Dr. Cummins?

     8. I don't know why they use plutonium* to generate electricity.

     9. Why don't we go to that resort* in the mountains this weekend?

    10. I'm angry with my daughter.

    11. I don't think you should take so many painkillers*.

    12. It seems the accident wasn't too bad.

a. It's known to remain dangerous for many years.

b. It's expected to stop soon, though.

c. You're only supposed to take it with food.

d. There's supposed to be a lot to do there.

e. They're not supposed to be good for your liver*.

f. She is said to have stolen money.

g. She was supposed to wash the dishes, but she didn't.

✔ h. You're supposed to be at work.

i. She's supposed to be very good.

j. No one was reported to have been seriously injured.

k. It's supposed to be very good.

l. She is believed to have food and water, fortunately.

* candidate: *a person competing for a political office or in some other election*
* plutonium: *a radioactive chemical element*
* resort: *a place where people go for sports and relaxation*
* painkillers: *pills that reduce pain*
* liver: *a large organ in the body that cleans the blood*

Have something done

Complete the conversations. Use the correct form of *have something done* with the words in parentheses.

1. *A:* Why is Jeremy going to the barber again so soon? He was there last week.

   B: (his head / shave) He wants to ___*have his head shaved*___ .

2. *A:* Is your sister's surgery serious?

   B: Not at all. (a mole* / remove) She just wants to _____ .

3. *A:* What should we do about these crank telephone calls*?

   B: (our telephone number / change) I think we should _____ .

4. *A:* Is Ashley's hair naturally curly?

   B: (her hair / perm*) No, she _____ twice a year.

5. *A:* I think the brakes in your car need to be looked at.

   B: You're right. (the brakes / check) I'm going to _____
   next week.

6. *A:* Why are you going to the dentist? You don't have a toothache, do you?

   B: (my teeth / clean) No, I am just going to_____ .

7. *A:* I can't pick up your prescription* until after work. Can you wait that long?

   B: (the prescription / deliver) That's all right. I'll _____
   this morning.

* mole: *a small, permanent dark spot on the skin*
* crank telephone call: *a call intended to bother or trick someone*
* perm: *to treat hair chemically to make it curly*
* prescription: *medicine ordered by a doctor for a patient*

REVIEW
Passive

Read the paragraphs. Mark the statements _T_ for true or _F_ for false. Correct the false statements.

A

Friday is payday for Julie, and she is always happy when she gets her paycheck. However, she doesn't make very much money, and she has a lot of things to pay for. She gives a little money to her parents for food every week even though they don't ask her to. She is a salesperson at a big department store, and she buys lots of things there: clothes, shoes, luggage. Sometimes she doesn't use the things she buys. Julie's dad tells her she shouldn't buy the things she doesn't need, and she doesn't like to hear that. She thinks she should be able to spend her money the way she wants to. Her ten-year-old car is also a big expense. It often needs repairs. Julie is trying to save a little money for college because she will have to pay the tuition. She has a lot of responsibilities for a nineteen-year-old.

_T_ 1. Julie gets paid every week. _____

_F_ 2. She is paid quite well. _She isn't paid very well._ _____

_____ 3. Julie helps pay for food at home without being asked. _____

_____ 4. Most of her salary gets put in the bank. _____

_____ 5. Julie doesn't like being told how to spend her money. _____

_____ 6. Julie's car doesn't get repaired very often. _____

_____ 7. Julie's college tuition will be paid for by her parents. _____

B

Sally was born in a small town. Her parents wanted her to get the best education possible, and they didn't think the local high school was very good. So Sally's parents sent her to a boarding school* when she was thirteen even though it was very expensive for them. The boarding school was far away in a big city. Sally didn't like it. She missed her parents and life in her hometown. She didn't like living in a dorm* or sharing a room, and she especially didn't like the school telling her when to study and when to go to bed. Now, after two years at the boarding school, she likes it better. She participates in several sports and the drama club. She has friends who ask her to go places and do things with them. Now Sally is happy where she is.

_____ 1. At thirteen, Sally was sent away to boarding school. _____

_____ 2. Sally went there because she was offered a scholarship*. _____

_____ 3. Sally was given her own room at school. _____

_____ 4. She didn't like being told when she should study or go to bed. _____

_____ 5. Sally never gets invited anywhere. _____

* boarding school: _a school at which students live_
* dorm (dormitory): _a building where students live at a school_
* scholarship: _money given to somebody to pay for their education_

UNIT
44

Reported Speech (*He said that . . .*)

Reported Speech

Read what Kevin said to Don on the phone. Then write what Don told Maggie about his conversation with Kevin. Use reported speech.

✓1a. I can't go to the baseball game with you this Saturday.

✓1b. I'll be out of town.

1c. I have to go to Toronto.

2. I don't need the book I lent Maggie because I've already read it.

Kevin   Don

3. My son is going to paint my house for me.

4. My family is doing well.

5. My father was sick, but he's much better now.

6. I really enjoyed Maggie's cookies.

7. I'll see you next Saturday.

Don

Maggie

1. *Maggie:* Is Kevin going to go out with us?

   Don: No. He said <u>*(that) he couldn't go to the baseball game with us this Saturday*</u> .
   Maggie: Why not?

   Don: He said <u>*(that) he would be out of town*</u>   .
   Maggie: On business?

   Don: I'm not sure. He only said that _____ .

2. *Maggie:* Does Kevin want his book back?

   Don: No, he said _____ the book because _____ .

3. *Maggie:* Does he need any help painting his house?

   Don: No, he said _____ .

4. *Maggie:* How's his family?

   Don: He said _____ .

5. *Maggie:* Did he say anything about his father?

   Don: Yes. He said _____ .

6. *Maggie:* Did he eat the cookies I made for him?

   Don: Yes. He said _____ .

7. *Maggie:* When will we see him?

   Don: He said _____ .

Reported Speech (*He said that . . .*)

Read the sentences in direct speech. Then use them to complete the sentences with reported speech.

> Please don't tell anyone what I said.

> ✔You look just like your grandfather.

> You have a very nice accent in English.

> Take it easy and relax.

> ✔Please don't forget to call me back.

> I've been very busy at work lately.

> Please hold for a minute.

> You'll have to help out more at home.

> You don't have to bring a present to the birthday party.

> My brother is selling his house.

1. Jason needs a friend's address urgently, so he asked *me not to forget to call him back* .

2. My grandmother once told me that *I looked just like my grandfather* OR *I look . . .* .

3. I tried to encourage the new French student by telling him _____
   _____ .

4. Brian was very upset with a coworker of ours, so I told him _____
   _____ .

5. Jane and her husband want to buy a house. I told _____ .

6. The doctor was with a patient when I called. The nurse asked _____
   _____ .

7. When I turned sixteen, my father told _____ .

8. Nicholas apologized for not getting in touch*. He said _____ .

9. Sally is afraid of her boss. After she told me about her problems at work, she asked
   _____ .

10. When she called to invite me, Emily said that _____
    _____ .

* get in touch with someone: *to contact someone (by phone, E-mail, etc.)*

EXERCISE 62

Reported Speech

Read the paragraph in which a man tells about his conversation with his sister-in-law*. Then change the reported speech to direct speech. Use the words in parentheses and any other necessary words. Be sure to use quotation marks and other necessary punctuation.

My sister-in-law Mona called to complain about her husband, who is my brother. She said my brother was spending too much time at work. Then she told me he wasn't very responsible about money. She said he often spent money on himself instead of on her and the children. She asked me not to tell my brother about our conversation. I told her not to worry, that I wouldn't say anything to him. I advised her to speak to him frankly* but not to get angry while they were discussing these matters. I said her anger would make him reluctant* to talk openly. She said she would try to follow my advice.

1. (spending / work)

   Mona said, " *Your brother is spending too much time at work* ."

2. (responsible / money)

   She said, "He _____."

3. (money / himself / children)

   She said, _____

4. (not / conversation)

   She said, "Please _____

5. (worry) (say anything)

   I said, _____

6. (frankly) (angry / matters)

   I said, _____, but _____

7. (anger / talk openly)

   I said, _____

8. (try / advice)

   She said, _____

   * sister-in-law: *a brother's wife or a husband or wife's sister*
   * frankly: *honestly, directly*
   * reluctant: *slow or not willing (to do something)*

Look at what each person did. Read what each one says. Report what each person said, and then what each person really did.

1. Yesterday morning

2. Lunch time yesterday

3. Last week

4. Breakfast this morning

5. Last Thursday morning

6. Last week

No sé, pero es posible.

7. Last month

1. Martin: "I get up at six every morning."
   Martin said *he got up at six every morning* ,
   but he *didn't get up at six yesterday* .

2. Jason: "I haven't eaten anything all day."
   At dinner last night, Jason said *he hadn't eaten*
   anything all day , but *he ate* something at lunch
   time yesterday.

3. Sally: "I always cut my hair myself."
   Sally said _____ , but
   _____ it herself last week.

4. Reggie: "I always eat a very small breakfast."
   Reggie said _____ ,
   _____ a lot this morning.

5. Jane: "I'm taking the bus to work Thursday morning."
   Jane said _____ ,
   _____ car to work that morning.

6. Jerry: "I don't know how to play a musical instrument."
   Jerry told me _____ ,
   _____ the guitar last week.

7. My teacher: "I can't speak Spanish."
   My teacher told us _____ ,
   but she _____ on the phone last month.

Questions

Make questions. Ask about the underlined words. Use question marks.

Statements	Questions
1. <u>Somebody important</u> visited my company today.	Who *visited your company today?*
2. We invited <u>some</u> people to our anniversary party.	How many *people did you invite to your anniversary party?*
3. <u>Some</u> people came to our party last weekend.	How many _____
4. I miss <u>someone</u> a lot.	Who _____
5. <u>Some</u> people were injured in the traffic accident.	How many _____
6. I have <u>some</u> good friends.	How many _____
7. <u>Someone's</u> child left behind this toy.	Whose child _____
8. Josephine is studying for <u>some</u> test.	Which test _____ _____ for?
9. I am best friends with <u>someone famous</u>.	Who _____ _____ with?
10. <u>Something unusual</u> occurs twice a month.	What _____
11. Roy lent me <u>some money</u>.	How much money _____
12. I have bought a house <u>somewhere unusual</u>.	Where _____
13. My grandmother was going to give me <u>something unusual</u> for my birthday.	What _____

NIT
46

Questions

Write questions for the answers. Read the answer first. Use the words in parentheses and any other necessary words. Put the verb in an appropriate tense.

Questions	Answers
1. (you / wait for) _Who are you waiting for?_	No one. I'm just waiting for the bus.
2. (not / want / to go swimming) _Don't you want to go swimming?_	No, I don't. It's too cold.
3. (you / have / this car) How _____ ?	Since 1998.
4. (not / go / to work yesterday) _____	Because I was sick.
5. (the children / listen to) _____	A new CD. Do you want me to ask them to turn the music down*?
6. (you / get up / tomorrow) _____	At seven, as usual.
7. (can / find / a good used car) _____	You can look in the newspaper. There are a lot for sale.
8. (not / feel / well) _____	Yes, I am. Why do you ask?
9. (your brother / do) _____	He's writing a letter.
10. (you / come / to this country) _____	Three years ago.
11. (you / meet / your husband) _____	A friend introduced us to each other.
12. (your teacher / born / in this country) _____	No, but she's a native speaker.
13. (these clothes / made) _____	I think they were made in China. Look at the labels*.

* turn down: *to lower, or decrease, the volume*
* label: *a piece of cloth on clothing with the size, instructions for cleaning, etc.*

Complete the conversations. Read the answers first. Use the words in parentheses and any other necessary words. Put the verb in an appropriate tense.

1. *Liz:* (that blue car / cost) Can you tell me <u>*how much that blue car costs*</u> ?
   Car salesperson: $7,500.

2. *William:* (the magazines and newspapers) I wonder if you could tell me _____
   _____ ?
   Librarian: They're on the second floor.

3. *Jim:* (that chicken / weigh) Could you tell me _____ ?
   Butcher: It weighs just over three pounds.

4. *Francis:* (to San Francisco) Do you have any idea _____ ?
   Friend: Pretty far. It's about 900 miles from here.

5. *Roger:* (Shakespeare / born) Do you remember _____ ?
   Classmate: In 1564. And he died in 1616.

6. *Linda:* (get / angry) I can't understand _____
      at me yesterday.
   Rick: Because you hurt my feelings!

7. *Jane:* ("diffident" / mean) Do you have any idea _____ ?
   Friend: Yes, it means "shy."

8. *Paul:* (Ashgabad / be) I have absolutely no idea _____ .
   Teacher: It's in Turkmenistan near the Caspian Sea.

Questions (*Do you know where . . . ? / She asked me where . . .*)

Read the questions in the box. Look at the people described in parentheses, and decide which question goes with which pair of speakers. Then use reported speech to write what the first person in the pair asked the second person.

> What time does the bus go to the airport?
> Why did the police officer give you a ticket*?
> Can you stay late to do some work?
> When are you going to turn in* the homework?
> How's the weather?
> Where do you have pain?
> ✔Do you have your driver's license?
> Will it hurt very much?
> Have you ever been to Hawaii?

1. (a police officer / me) *A police officer asked me whether I had my driver's license.*
   OR . . . if I had my driver's license.

2. (the teacher / Laura) The teacher asked Laura _____ .

3. (the doctor / Mr. Chen) _____

4. (her boss / Gloria) _____

5. (we / the hotel clerk) _____

6. (the travel agent / Mrs. White) _____

7. (the patient / the dentist) _____

8. (I / my friend on vacation in Florida) _____

9. (my father / me) _____

* ticket: *a notice from the police that you have broken a traffic law, e.g., a speeding ticket, a parking ticket*
* turn (something) in: *to give (something) to someone in authority*

Auxiliary verbs (*have/do/can*, etc.)   *I think so / I hope so*, etc.

**Complete the sentences. Use the words in parentheses and an appropriate verb.
Look at the second part of the sentence carefully.**

1. (olives / sweet) <u>*Olives aren't sweet*</u>, and neither are lemons.

2. (my brother / speak / Chinese) <u>*My brother speaks Chinese*</u>, but his wife doesn't.

3. (I / see / the new Canadian movie) _____, and neither has Ronald.

4. (I / very quiet) _____, and so are my neighbors.

5. (I / have / another piece of cake) _____, and neither should you.

6. (My brother / like / to cook) _____, and so does his wife.

7. (my friends / buy / a present for Maria) _____, but I did.

8. (Jeff / have to / take / a business trip) _____, and so did his brother.

9. (yesterday / cold) _____, but the day before was.

10. (my neighbors / on vacation) _____, and so are the Smiths.

11. (I / miss / a day of work) _____, and so can you.

12. (Chris / be / at the party) _____, but his girlfriend will.

13. (Sylvia / be / to Brazil) _____, but I haven't.

EXERCISE 69

Auxiliary verbs (*have/do/can*, etc.) *I think so / I hope so*, etc.

You're talking to a friend. Write true responses about yourself. If appropriate, use *so* or *neither* and the correct auxiliary verb. Look at the examples carefully.

Friend	**You**
1. I'd like something to eat.	*So would I.*
2. I'm too tired to go out tonight.	*You are? I'm not.*
3. I didn't have time to read the paper yesterday.	*Neither did I.*
4. I would like to go to Moscow.	
5. My sister likes chocolate a lot.	
6. I have never been to India.	
7. Mrs. Smith didn't eat dinner last night.	
8. I can't play a musical instrument.	
9. I was very hungry when I got up this morning.	
10. I'm not going to take any trips this month.	
11. I should sleep more.	
12. My brother has to go to summer school*.	
13. I watched a very interesting program on TV last night.	
14. I wasn't born in this country.	

* summer school: *classes that take place during summer vacation*

EXERCISE 70

Auxiliary verbs (*have/do/can*, etc.) *I think so / I hope not*, etc.

Read the sentences at the top. Then answer A's questions. Use the word in parentheses and *so* or *not*.

1. You don't like fish.
   A: Is Ted cooking fish for dinner?

   B: (hope) *I hope not.*

2. You are pretty sure the movie lasts only ninety minutes.
   A: The movie starts at 7 P.M. Will we be out by 9?

   B: (think) _____

3. Mark is usually off on Fridays.
   A: Is Mark working this Friday?

   B: (think) _____

4. Your electric bill is due today.
   A: Do we have to pay the electric bill today?

   B: (afraid) _____

5. You have very little extra money.
   A: Do you think I could borrow $20 till next week?

   B: (afraid) _____

6. You don't have any plans for Thursday night.
   A: Will you be home Thursday night?

   B: (guess) _____

7. The party started at 7 P.M., it's 9 P.M. now, and Alan hasn't come.
   A: Isn't Alan coming?

   B: (guess) _____

8. You already have plans for Friday night.
   A: Can you come over for dinner on Friday?

   B: (afraid) _____

9. The last time you checked, there was no sugar.
   A: Do we have any sugar?

   B: (think) _____

10. You don't like Matthew's cousin.
    A: Is Matthew bringing his cousin when he comes to see us?

    B: (hope) _____

11. Marge goes to church every Sunday.
    A: Do you think we'll see Marge in church?

    B: (suppose) _____

12. Jack is short of* money this year.
    A: Do you think Jack will take a long vacation this year?

    B: (suppose) _____

13. You love Chinese food.
    A: Are your parents taking us out for Chinese food?

    B: (hope) _____

* be short of (something): *not to have enough (money, time, etc.)*

UNIT
49

Tag Questions (*do you? / isn't it?*, etc.)

A. Add question tags (*do you?*, *isn't it?*, etc.) to these statements to make them tag questions. Use question marks.

1. The mail carrier is late today, *isn't he?*   Yes, a little.

2. You can give me a hand* tomorrow, _____   Yes, count on me.

3. You wouldn't have an extra dollar or two, _____   No, I'm broke*. Sorry.

4. Cheese should be kept in the refrigerator, _____ Yes, it should.

5. The Nelsons spend a lot of time away from home, _____   Yes, they travel a lot.

6. You wouldn't lend Zachary $100, _____   No, never.

7. Your brother's acting a little strange, _____   No, that's just how he is.

8. Matthew said he was coming to the party, _____   Yes, he did.

9. Your brother wishes he was married, _____   Yes, he does.

10. You won't forget to bring me the CD, _____   No, I won't.

* give someone a hand: *to help someone*
* broke: *without money*

EXERCISE CONTINUES ▶ ▶

B. Write the first part of the tag questions. Use the words in parentheses, put the verb in an appropriate form, and add any necessary words. Look at the question tag carefully first.

1. (Jennifer / make / plane reservations) _Jennifer has_ _made plane reservations_ , hasn't she? Yes, I think so.

2. (do / anything important) _____ _____ , were you? No, just watching TV.

3. (Hannah / like / her new job) _____ _____ , does she? Actually, she likes it a lot. Why?

4. (this shirt / expensive) _____ , isn't it? Yes, very expensive.

5. (use / your tools) _____ , can't I? Sure, go ahead.

6. (your shirt / made in the United States) _____ _____ , was it? No, in China.

7. (much milk left*) _____ , is there? No, we need to get more.

8. (finish / your homework) _____ , haven't you? Yes, I have.

* left: *remaining; for example, I only have five dollars left.*

Think of a person you want to meet. Write ten questions to ask that person. Include two tag questions and two questions that begin with *Do you know . . . ?* or *Can you tell me . . . ?*

Name of Person: *Paul McCartney*

1. *How did you become a Beatle?*
2. *You still write songs, don't you?*
3. *Can you tell me if you plan to do a concert tour?*

Name of Person: _____

1. _____ ?
2. _____ ?
3. _____ ?
4. _____ ?
5. _____ ?
6. _____ ?
7. _____ ?
8. _____ ?
9. _____ ?
10. _____ ?

UNIT
50

Verb + *-ing* (*enjoy doing / stop doing*, etc.)

Complete the sentences, keeping the same meaning. Use *-ing*.

1. The Petersons like to eat out.

   The Petersons enjoy _eating out_____ .

2. We have to do the shopping first; then we can go home.

   We can't go home until we finish _____ .

3. Don't interrupt me again, please.

   Would you please stop _____ ?

4. I can't work in that office anymore.

   I can't go on _____ office.

5. Does it bother you to live alone?

   Do you mind _____ ?

6. Luke isn't going to change jobs until next year.

   Luke is going to put off _____ .

7. Louise said, "Why don't we watch a video at home?"

   Louise suggested _____ .

8. Why does Josh tell the same stories about his dog over and over again*?

   Why does Josh keep _____ dog?

9. Sam doesn't care if we drive his car as long as we buy some gas.

   Sam doesn't mind us _____ .

10. Greg can't lift anything heavy until his back is better.

    Greg has to avoid _____ .

11. I used to walk to work every day, and I miss it now.

    I miss _____ day.

   * over and over again: *many times; repeatedly*

Verb + *to* . . . (*decide to do / forget to do*, etc.)

Read the conversations. Then complete the sentences with *to* + verb and any other necessary words. Some sentences require *not* or a question word (*what, whether, how*, etc.).

Did you remember to mail my package?

No, I didn't. Sorry.

1. *He* forgot *to mail her package* .

Did you finally get a raise at work?

Yes, I finally did. I kept asking for a raise until I got one.

2. She finally managed _____ .

It really hurts me when you call me "stupid."

I'm sorry. I won't do it again.

3. _____ promised _____ .

Can I give you a ride home?

That's all right. I have my car.

4. _____ offered _____ .

Please don't tell anyone what I said.

Don't worry. I won't.

5. He agreed _____ .

EXERCISE CONTINUES ▶ ▶

Are you going to visit your family this Christmas?

No, I don't have enough money.

6. _____ can't afford _____ .

Should we buy a new car?

No, I don't think that's a good idea right now.

I guess you're right.

7. They decided _____ .

Josh, you'd look nice with short hair. Why don't you get a haircut?

I don't want to. I like it long.

8. _____ refused _____ .

I don't know whether I should go to Canada or to Mexico on vacation.

Why don't you come and look at my pictures? I'll help you decide.

9. _____ couldn't decide _____ .

_____ promised _____

Can I have a day off tomorrow?

I don't see why not if you finish all your work today.

I will.

10. He arranged _____ .

How can I get to the airport at five tomorrow morning?

Call a taxi tonight and arrange to be picked up at four.

11. _____ explained to her _____ .

Verb + -ing (enjoy doing / stop doing, etc.)
Verb + to . . . (decide to do / forget to do, etc.)
Verb + (Object) + to . . . (I want to do / I want you to do, etc.)

Complete the sentences with the correct form of the verb in parentheses. Use the base form, to + verb, or verb + -ing. Some sentences require not.

1. Helen suggested _____*going*_____ (go) to a Chinese restaurant, but we decided
   ___*to try*___ (try) a new Mexican place instead.

2. "You'd be healthier if you quit _____ (smoke) ," said the doctor.

3. Don't worry. I've arranged for my brother _____ (pick) you up
   at the airport tomorrow.

4. I can't afford _____ (eat) at expensive restaurants because
   I'm not working now.

5. Would you mind _____ (play) your trumpet in the house?

6. I wouldn't go out with wet hair. You risk _____ (catch) a cold.

7. My boss expects us _____ (get) to work on time; she also expects us
   _____ (waste) time talking to coworkers about personal matters.

8. Angela is letting her hair _____ (grow) long.

9. The park doesn't allow _____ (swim) in the pond*, but it does
   allow people _____ (fish) there with a license.

10. We were warned _____ (walk) in that part of the city after dark.

11. Mr. Chism is a strict father. He makes his children _____ (do)
    work around the house or in the yard.

12. If I forget, remind me _____ (feed) the cat before we leave.

13. Hannah had a headache, but she went on _____ (study) anyway.

14. Mr. Jones threatened _____ (stop) cooking because his wife kept
    _____ (complain) about the meals he fixed.

15. I couldn't get the store _____ (give) me a refund* for the sweater
    I wanted to return.

* pond: *a small area of water*
* refund: *a sum of money paid back*

Verb + *-ing* or *to . . . (remember/regret*, etc.)
Verb + *-ing* or *to . . . (try/need/help)*

Complete the sentences with *to* + verb or verb + *-ing*. Use an appropriate verb.

1. After getting her bachelor's degree* in history, Susan went on _to study_ journalism at another university.

2. Max doesn't remember _calling_ the police after the accident, but I heard him make the call.

3. I should have bought my holiday presents sooner. I regret not _____ them when the stores were less crowded.

4. I can't help _____ when I see Ted. I always think of the funny joke he told us.

5. Mrs. Brown thinks she'll go on _____ at the library until she retires*.

6. The stain* on my shirt is gone. I tried _____ lemon juice on the stain, and it worked.

7. Before I leave town, I have to remember _____ my suit from the cleaner's.

8. If one aspirin doesn't help your toothache, try _____ two aspirins every four hours.

9. I am starting _____ a little better now with the new medicine I'm taking.

10. Don't you remember _____ my boss at our party last year? She was the one who kept asking you questions about computers.

11. My doctor told me I need _____ a lot of juice and tea until my cold is better.

12. You are very upset because of the accident. Try _____ and tell me what happened.

13. Our history teacher discussed the American Revolution. Then he went on _____ the American Civil War with us.

* bachelor's degree: *a four-year university degree, e.g., B.A., B.S.*
* retire: *to stop working, often because of reaching a particular age, such as sixty-five*
* stain: *a dirty mark, usually on clothing, that is difficult to remove*

NITS   # Verb -*ing* or *to* . . . (*try/need/help*)
4-55   # Verb -*ing* or *to* . . . (*like / would like*, etc.)

Combine the two sentence halves to make meaningful sentences. Write the letter of the second half next to the first half.

<table>
<tr><td>

A

_c_ 1. I'd really love

____ 2. I have always liked

____ 3. I can't stand

____ 4. If your computer won't start up*, first try

____ 5. Phil is going to sell his old car. He has tried

____ 6. I'm not ready to let my teenager drive by herself. The matter needs

____ 7. Nicholas seems to hate

____ 8. I'm sorry I missed that Australian film. I would really like

____ 9. I was wondering if you could help me

____10. Most people can't help

____11. I would like my sister

____12. Please believe me. I honestly don't mind

</td><td>

B

a. to be less bossy*.

b. to fix it many times, but it still doesn't run right.

✔c. to take a month off from work.

d. understand the words to this song.

e. waiting for you if you won't be long.

f. to have seen it.

g. feeling sad once in a while*.

h. getting up early even when I don't have to.

i. to be discussed some more.

j. living with his new roommate.

k. checking if it's plugged in properly.

l. waiting in line for a long time at the post office.

</td></tr>
</table>

* start up: *to begin working or running*
* bossy: *fond of giving orders*
* once in a while: *occasionally, sometimes*

Complete the sentences, keeping the same meaning.

1. Robbie likes iced tea more than hot tea.

    Robbie would rather *drink iced tea than hot tea*   .

2. Robbie likes iced tea more than hot tea.

    Robbie prefers iced tea *to hot tea*   .

3. Fred would rather live on a boat than in a house.

    Fred prefers *living*   on a boat to *living in a house*   .

4. Are you going to make dinner, or should I?

     Are you going to make dinner or would you rather I *made it*   ?

5. I like eating at home better than in a restaurant.

    I'd rather _____ .

6. I don't like to drive other people's cars.

    I'd rather not _____ .

7. Would you prefer to stay home rather than go out tonight?

    Would you rather _____ ?

8. Christine doesn't want to visit Las Vegas on her vacation; she wants to visit Puerto Rico.

    Christine prefers Puerto Rico _____ for her vacation.

9. Some shoppers would rather have their purchases* delivered than carry them home themselves.

    Some shoppers prefer _____ to _____ .

10. Your German is better than mine. You should translate the letter into English.

    I'd rather you _____ .

11. Are you going to call George, or should I?

    _____ , or would you rather I _____ ?

12. I'd prefer that you not tell anyone what I said.

    I'd rather you _____ .

    * purchase: *something bought*

Preposition (*in/for/about*, etc.) + *-ing*

Complete the sentences, keeping the same meaning. Use a verb + *-ing*.

1. Let's not go to a restaurant. Let's cook something at home instead.

   Let's *cook something at home* instead of *going to a restaurant* .

2. How does Andrew expect to do well in school? He doesn't make an effort.

   How _____ without _____ ?

3. My teacher told me to improve my pronunciation. She said to listen to native speakers.

   My teacher _____ by _____ .

4. I'm leaving town on business next week. I have a lot to do before then.

   I have _____ before _____ .

5. I'm having dinner at my favorite restaurant tonight. I'm looking forward to it.

   I am looking forward to _____ .

6. Pam runs five miles every day. That's why her leg is sore*.

   Pam's leg is sore from _____ .

7. I'd like to go to a Japanese restaurant tonight. How do you feel about that?

   How do you feel about _____ ?

8. Amy's lonely because it's difficult for her to make friends.

   Amy _____ because she isn't good at _____ .

9. We might go to Toronto next weekend. Are you interested?

   _____ interested in _____ ?

10. I found the restaurant, and nobody gave me directions.

    _____ without anybody _____ .

11. Sarah went to work this morning even though she had to drive on snow and ice.

    Sarah _____ in spite of _____ .

   * sore: *painful and uncomfortable*

EXERCISE 80

Be / get used to something (*I'm used to . . .*)

Read the passage about Alice's first year at college. Put the verbs in parentheses in the correct form.

When Alice first went away to college last September, she wasn't used to **1)** _taking_ (take) care of herself. It was the first time she had lived away from her parents, so she was very homesick in the beginning. At home, she used to **2)** _have_ (have) her own room, so she wasn't used to **3)** _____ (share) an apartment with another person at first. It took her a few months to get used to **4)** _____ (live) with her college roommate.

When she was in high school, her parents used to **5)** _____ (remind) her to do her homework and **6)** _____ (make) decisions for her. In college, she had to get used to **7)** _____ (be) more independent. No one reminds her to study, and she has to make her own decisions. Her high school classes were easy. In college, she had to get used to **8)** _____ (study) very hard – two hours or more for every hour of class.

In high school, Alice used to **9)** _____ (drive) her parents' car when she needed to go somewhere. In college, she is now used to **10)** _____ (ride) a bike and **11)** _____ (take) the bus. At home, Alice's mother used to **12)** _____ (do) all the shopping, cooking, and cleaning. Alice didn't use to **13)** _____ (help) out much. At college, she had to get used to **14)** _____ (be) more responsible. Actually, she and her roommate share these jobs, but Alice always does her part.

Now, when Alice goes home to visit, she often helps her mother around the house. Although she appreciates the help, it is often hard for Alice's mother to accept it because she is used to **15)** _____ (do) everything herself at home. Alice's mother is slowly getting used to **16)** _____ (let) her daughter help her, however. It's a pleasure for her to see Alice turning into a responsible, independent adult.

Verb + Preposition + -ing (succeed in -ing / accuse somebody of -ing, etc.)

N I T
59

Complete the sentences. Use the correct preposition and an appropriate verb + -ing. Some sentences require an object pronoun (me, him, them, etc.) and some require not.

1. I've been thinking _of buying_ a new TV, but I don't know where to buy it.

2. Ann accused _me of lying_ OR _me of not telling the truth_, but I swear* I told her the truth.

3. Do you feel _____ to a movie, or would you rather stay home?

4. I wouldn't dream _____ your car without asking you first.

5. Excuse _____ here on time. I had trouble with my car again.

6. I think we should apologize _____ your brother's birthday.
   We didn't remember to call or send a card.

7. I'm not looking forward _____ my speech in front of class next week.
   I always get nervous.

8. When I travel with Ben, he always insists _____ at the best hotels.

9. I hope you succeed _____ a nice apartment. I know you've been
   looking for one for a long time.

10. What prevented the fire department _____ to the fire more quickly?
    It took the fire truck almost twenty minutes to get there.

11. My daughter is eighteen, so I can't stop _____ her friends even if
    I don't like them.

12. I am thinking _____ to Argentina. Have you ever been there?

13. Do those children watch too much TV? Do you think the TV keeps

    _____ their homework?

14. I'd like to congratulate you _____ promoted to manager
    in your company.

15. Sarah is the most honest person I know. How can you accuse _____
    dishonest?

  * swear: _to promise very seriously to tell the truth_

UNIT
60

Expressions + -ing

Complete the sentences, keeping the same meaning. Use -ing.

1. There's nothing you can do about your brother's divorce. Don't worry about it.

   It's no use _worrying about your brother's divorce_ .

2. I liked the movie and think others should see it too.

   That movie is worth _seeing_ .

3. It's not easy for him to apologize to people.

   He has trouble _____ .

4. I wouldn't keep that old magazine if I were you.

   There's no point in _____ .

5. You really shouldn't spend so much time watching TV.

   It's a waste of time _____ .

6. Let's not drive across town just to buy lemons.

   It's not worth _____ .

7. Don't bother* calling Mary Jo. She won't answer the phone.

   It's no use _____ because she won't
   answer the phone.

8. It was very hard for me to reach my uncle by phone.

   I had a lot of trouble _____ .

9. Margie goes to the store twice a week.

   Margie goes _____ .

10. Don't bother inviting Emily to the party. She won't be in town then.

    There's no point in _____ because she
    will be out of town then.

11. Lee fixed his car from 8 A.M. till 3 P.M. yesterday.

    Lee spent seven _____ .

   * bother: *to make the effort to do something*

To . . . , for . . . , and so that . . . (Purpose)

Complete the sentences, keeping the same meaning.

1. We are going to the mountains so that we can enjoy the cool weather.

    We are going to the mountains to _enjoy the cool weather_____ .

2. I drove Colin downtown for his driving test.

    I drove Colin downtown so that _he could take his driving test_____ .

3. Josh went to the store to get some milk.

    Josh went to the store for _some milk_____ .

4. We left early – we didn't want to miss the bus.

    We left early so that _____ .

5. I sat down so that I could try on some shoes.

    I sat down to _____ .

6. Let's take a break* to have some lunch.

    Let's take a break for _____ .

7. Sandy wrote a note to herself. She didn't want to forget to stop at the bank after work.

    Sandy wrote a note to herself so that _____ .

8. I gave Tim five dollars for some groceries.

    I gave Tim five dollars so that _____ .

9. Stan is saving his money so that he can take a trip to Finland.

    Stan is saving his money for _____ .

10. They closed the store early. They wanted the employees to be able to spend the holiday with their families.

    They closed the store early so that _____ .

11. Mr. Perkins needs an operation so that he can walk again.

    Mr. Perkins needs an operation to _____ .

    * take a break: *to take a rest*

Adjective + *to*
To . . . (*afraid to do*) and Preposition + *-ing* (*afraid of -ing*)

A. Complete the sentences. Use *to* + verb and information from a sentence in List 1.

1. I was sorry *to hear about your father's accident* .

2. I was relieved _____ .

3. I was very pleased _____ .

4. I was quite surprised _____ .

5. I was pretty disappointed _____ .

List 1
    a. I saw you on TV last week.
    b. I heard your brother finally got out of the hospital.
✔c. I heard about your father's accident.
    d. I met your parents the other night.
    e. I learned I didn't get the job.

B. Complete the sentences. Use *of* . . . and *to* + verb and information from a sentence in List 2.

1. It was extravagant* *of the Bonds to spend a month's salary in one weekend* .

2. It was kind _____ .

3. It was pretty careless _____ .

4. It was unfair _____ .

5. It was clever _____ .

List 2
    a. You thought of others before yourself.
    b. Carlos went to bed with the doors open.
    c. Maria convinced the police officer not to give her a ticket*.
    d. We formed an opinion* of the woman before meeting her.
✔e. The Bonds spent a month's salary in one weekend.

* extravagant: *spending more money than is necessary*
* ticket: *a notice from the police that you have broken a traffic law, e.g., a speeding ticket, a parking ticket*
* form an opinion of someone: *to make a decision about the person's character*

EXERCISE CONTINUES ▶ ▶

C. Complete the sentences with items from List 3. Use the items in the list as they are without changing them.

1. I admire Sarah's honesty. She's not afraid <u>*to tell people what she thinks*</u> .

2. Kathy is afraid _____ because she asked him for some last week.

3. She is afraid _____ .

4. I'm sorry _____ , but someone wants you on the phone.

5. I'm sorry _____ . I didn't know you were talking to someone.

6. I'm interested _____ . I like action movies.

7. I'll be interested _____ after you see it.

List 3
   a. in seeing that new Chinese movie
   b. to interrupt you
   ✔c. to tell people what she thinks
   d. of being turned down*
   e. to know what you think of the movie
   f. for interrupting your conversation this morning
   g. to ask her father for money

   * turn down: *to refuse*

-ing and the Infinitive Units 50–65   **91**

UNIT
64

See somebody do and see somebody doing

Complete the sentences. Use an appropriate verb.

1. A lot of people say Gloria is a gossip*, but I haven't actually heard her _say_ anything bad about anybody.

2. On the way home from work, I saw my neighbor Fred _cutting_ his grass in the rain.

3. Did you hear them _____ your name on the radio yesterday?

4. I didn't actually see Helen _____ , but they say she fell and hurt herself at work yesterday.

5. Listen. Can you hear air _____ from this tire?

6. When I was leaving home this morning, I noticed a stranger _____ on my neighbor's door.

7. I didn't hear Alex _____ his new song because I couldn't go to the concert.

8. Kevin got angry at his sister because he found her _____ his new sweater.

9. Ted can't be very sick. I saw him _____ in a restaurant last night.

10. Why do you think I took your pen? Did you see me _____ it?

11. Could you look out the window and tell me if you see a taxi _____ ? I called one twenty minutes ago.

12. Fred is a very patient person. In five years I have never seen him _____ angry.

13. When I got home, I could smell food _____ on the stove. It made me hungry.

14. As I was leaving the doctor's office, I heard the doctor and nurse _____ about my case.

  * gossip: *a person who likes to talk about other people*

-ing Phrases (*Feeling tired, I went to bed early.*)

Join the two sentences by making the italicized one an -*ing* phrase. Sometimes the -*ing* phrase needs *having* or *not*. Look at the examples carefully.

The sentences are about what happened after you hurt your arm.

1. I hurt my arm. / *I helped a friend fix his car yesterday.*

    I hurt my arm helping a friend fix his car yesterday.

2. *I hoped that she could relieve* the pain.* / I went to the doctor.

    Hoping that she could relieve my pain, I went to the doctor.

3. *I had arrived late in the day without an appointment.* / I had to wait to see the doctor.

    Having arrived late in the day without an appointment, I had to wait to see the doctor.

4. I had to wait a long time. / *I sat in agony*.*

    _____

5. The doctor gave me a prescription* for a painkiller*. / *She promised it would work fast.*

    _____

6. *I didn't know that they would upset my stomach.* / I took the pills without food.

    _____

7. *He had left me at the doctor's earlier.* / My friend came to my house to see me last night.

    _____

8. I woke up this morning. *I felt much better.*

    _____

* relieve: *to make less bad*
* agony: *extreme physical or mental suffering*
* prescription: *medicine ordered by a doctor for a patient*
* painkiller: *pill that reduces pain*

EXERCISE 87

-ing and the Infinitive

Use your own ideas to write sentences with the words in parentheses. Put the second verb in the appropriate form: verb + *-ing*, *to* + verb, or base form.

1. (can afford / buy) _I can afford to buy a new car, but I don't need one._
   Many people who can't afford to buy a new car get a loan from the bank.
   My brother couldn't afford to buy a house last spring because he had just
   gotten married.

2. (can't help / cry) _I can't help crying when I see sad movies._
   My parents couldn't help crying when I left home for college.
   Many American parents can't helping crying a little when a child gets married.

3. (would rather / eat) _____

4. (threaten / stop) _____

5. (regret / not do) _____

6. (warn / spend) _____

7. (prefer / work) _____

8. (go on / talk) _____

9. (can't stand / be) _____

10. (mind / wait) _____

11. (deny / take) _____

12. (pretend / listen) _____

13. (imagine / wear) _____

EXERCISE CONTINUES ▶ ▶

14. (remember / do) _____

15. (try / act) _____

16. (advise / work) _____

17. (make / do) _____

18. (not / allow / use) _____

19. (need / remember) _____

20. (would like / have to) _____

21. (let / drive) _____

**Complete the passage with the verb in parentheses in the correct form: verb + *-ing*,
to + verb, or base form.**

A friend of mine, Judy, is thinking of **1)** <u>*working*</u> (work) abroad for two years. She
hasn't decided whether **2)** <u>*to look*</u> (look) for a job in Asia or in South America. She has
always wanted **3)** _____ (visit) both places. Judy regrets not **4)** _____ (take) a
foreign language in college, and she hopes that it will not prevent her from **5)** _____ (get)
a job in another country. A friend advised her **6)** _____ (decide) where she would like
7) _____ (go) first. Then she can learn as much of the language of the country as possible
before **8)** _____ (leave) on her trip. There's no point in **9)** _____ (study)
Chinese if she goes to Chile, is there? She needs **10)** _____ (know) where she is going
to move before she learns a language. She is a physical therapist*, so of course, she can't expect
11) _____ (help) patients if she doesn't speak their language.

Judy is a flexible*, intelligent person. I don't think she will have trouble **12)** _____ (get)
used to life in another country. I have to say that I can't help **13)** _____ (feel) a little
jealous of her. I would love **14)** _____ (live) abroad, too, but I would rather
15) _____ (go) to the Middle East. I have dreamt of **16)** _____ (visit) Egypt
and Turkey since I was little. I can't leave my job now, though. I will have to put off
17) _____ (travel) for at least three years.

  * physical therapist: *a person who is trained to use exercises, massage, etc., to treat injuries*
  * flexible: *able to change to fit different situations*

REVIEW

-ing and the Infinitive

Use your own ideas to complete each sentence. Use an appropriate verb in the correct form: verb + *-ing*, *to* + verb, or the base form. Use any other words that you need.

1. On their next vacation, my friends are looking forward to _going to the Czech Republic_ .
   On their next vacation, my friends are looking forward to _____ .

2. I am studying English _to get a better job_ _____ .
   I am studying English _____ .

3. Yesterday, I was surprised to hear _a young person use very rude* language_ _____ .
   Yesterday, I was surprised to hear _____ .

4. When I go to a new place, it's never easy for me to get used to _____ .

5. I'm used to _____ , but I will never get used to _____ .

6. At the end of a busy day, I sometimes feel like _____ .

7. I need to thank _____ for _____ .

8. Nothing can keep me from _____ .

9. A friend of mine spends a lot of time _____ .

10. When I have free time, I like to go _____ .

11. It is not thoughtful of people _____ .

12. When I was little, I was afraid _____ .

13. As for the future, I'm interested in _____ .

14. I have never seen anyone _____ .

15. One day I hope to hear _____ .

16. Not _____ , I have trouble _____ .

17. After _____ , I sometimes _____ .

   * rude: *not polite; behaving in a way that hurts other people's feelings*

UNITS
66-67

Countable and Uncountable Nouns

Answer the questions using the words in the lists. Add *a/an* or *-s* when necessary.

1. Which of these does a person need on a trip by car? Which doesn't a person need?

   airline ticket, gas, spare tire, tool, flashlight, suitcase, computer, map, time

   a. On a trip a person needs _gas, a spare tire, tools, a flashlight, suitcases_
      (OR a suitcase), a map (OR maps), and time .

   b. A person doesn't need _an airline ticket or a computer_ .

2. Which of these are good in a salad? Which aren't good?

   black pepper, butter, garlic, jam, lemon juice, lettuce, mushroom, oil, olive, piece of onion, banana, salt, tomato

   a. _____

      _____ are good in a salad.

   b. _____ aren't good in a salad.

3. Which of these are useful to a soccer player? Which are not useful?

   experience, good coach, strong arm and leg, healthy lung, long hair, rainy weather, time to practice, umbrella

   a. _____

      _____ are useful to a soccer player.

   b. _____ are not useful.

4. Which of these do the parents of a new baby need? Which don't they need?

   baby clothes, good doctor, help from relatives, information about vaccinations*, money, truck, new living room furniture, spare room

   a. The parents of a new baby need _____

      _____ .

   b. They don't need _____ .

5. Which of these does a person need to be healthy? Which are not necessary for good health?

   alcohol, car, clean water, coffee, enough sleep, expensive doctor, exercise, fresh air, good food, hard job, stress, tobacco

   a. To be healthy, a person needs _____

      _____ .

   b. _____ are not necessary for good health.

   * vaccination: *protection against disease (e.g., polio) by an injection*

EXERCISE 91

Countable and Uncountable Nouns

Complete the sentences. Use the words and phrases in the box. Sometimes you need *a/an* or the plural (-*s*).

hair	hard work	room	big suitcase
bad luck	bread	suggestion	trip
~~good news~~	good progress	permission	very good advice
~~job~~	luggage	room	view

1. I have _good news_ . My brother got _a job_ in Australia.

2. Can I make _____ ? I think we should stop for gas.

3. Gloria gave me _____ about my car.

4. Poor Frank. _____ seems to follow him.

5. You can't make a sandwich. We don't have _____ .

6. In school, students must ask for _____ to leave the room.

7. Jan and Steve rented the apartment because it has _____ of the river.

8. Now that her children live on their own, Mrs. Philips rents _____ to three or four students.

9. You're making _____ in math. It's because of your _____ , I think.

10. The trunk of my car has _____ for four _____ .

11. Mr. Gomez is over eighty, but he still has lots of nice white _____ .

12. Barbara bought _____ for _____ to Korea next month.

UNITS
66-70

Countable and Uncountable Nouns
Countable Nouns with *a/an* and *some*
A/an and *the*

Complete the passage about shopping at a supermarket with *a/an*, *the*, or *some*. Write *X* if none of these is possible.

There is a huge supermarket near my house called **1)** _X_ Jones's Market. **2)** _The_
supermarket is open 24 hours **3)** _a_ day, seven days **4)** _____ week, so I can shop
whenever I feel like it. When I go shopping for **5)** _____ food, I usually take my cart to
6) _____ produce section first because I eat a lot of fresh fruit and **7)** _____ vegetables.
I buy **8)** _____ meat, but not very much. Yesterday, I bought **9)** _____ whole chicken and
10) _____ pound of ground beef. I froze **11)** _____ beef to use later, but I'll cook
12) _____ chicken tonight. From **13)** _____ dairy section, I usually buy **14)** _____ dozen eggs
and **15)** _____ milk, but I don't buy **16)** _____ cheese.

I get a lot of things from **17)** _____ Aisle 6: **18)** _____ bag of **19)** _____ rice, **20)** _____ dry
beans, and usually **21)** _____ package or two of **22)** _____ pasta. I try to move down
23) _____ Aisle 5 very quickly so that I won't be tempted by **24)** _____ cookies there.
I buy **25)** _____ bread, of course, but not **26)** _____ kind in Aisle 5. I prefer **27)** _____ kind
of bread they sell in **28)** _____ bakery section of **29)** _____ store. I don't usually go down
30) _____ beverage* aisle because I don't like **31)** _____ soft drinks. But I do go down
32) _____ breakfast-food aisle to get **33)** _____ cereal for **34)** _____ breakfast.

I love **35)** _____ snack foods but try not to buy any because they're pretty expensive and
fattening*. **36)** _____ frozen foods also tend to be expensive, but I can't resist ice cream,
and I drink quite a lot of **37)** _____ frozen juice.

I like to do my food shopping early in the morning or late at night because there are fewer
shoppers in **38)** _____ store then.

* beverage: *a drink*
* fattening: *containing a lot of calories (of food) that makes people gain weight*

The (school / the school)
The (children / the children)
The (giraffe / the telephone / the piano, etc.; the + Adjective)

Put in *the* where necessary. If *the* is not necessary, write X.

1. __X__ Dinosaurs are extinct* but they have been __the__ subject of many recent films and books.

2. It is a country's responsibility to take care of _____ poor.

3. _____ young children are often more honest about their feelings than _____ most adults.

4. Jenny became a veterinarian because she loves _____ animals a lot.

5. _____ life of a doctor is usually a very busy one.

6. _____ life in the previous century was more difficult in many ways than _____ life is today.

7. Alex isn't paid for _____ work he does. He's a volunteer.

8. _____ most Americans take _____ work very seriously, perhaps too seriously.

9. Paul has been in _____ school for twenty years! Will he ever finish?

10. A neighbor of mine believes very strongly in taking _____ vitamins and eating _____ local fruit and vegetables rather than imported ones.

11. *A:* Which high school did you go to?

    B: _____ high school near _____ church on Main Street.

12. I love _____ classical music, especially pieces which feature _____ violin.

13. I know that _____ fish is good for you, but _____ fish we had last night didn't taste very good.

14. Now that Claudia has finished _____ high school, is she planning to go on to _____ college?

15. _____ couples who can't agree about whether to have _____ children probably shouldn't get married to each other.

16. Which invention was more important – _____ car or _____ computer?

* extinct: *no longer in existence*

UNITS
74-75

Names with and without *the*

Answer the questions about the pairs in parentheses. Include *the* where necessary. If you're not sure of the answer, begin with *I think*.

1. Which newspaper has more readers? (*New York Times* / *Wall Street Journal*)

   (I think) *The New York Times* has more readers than *The Wall Street Journal* .

2. Which is higher? (Empire State Building / Andes Mountains)

   _____ higher than _____ .

3. Which is busier? (O'Hare Airport in Chicago / Rhine-Main Airport in Frankfurt)

   _____ busier than _____ .

4. Which country has more people? (China / India)

   _____

5. Which country has a larger area? (Mexico / Dominican Republic)

   _____

6. Which area has a cooler climate? (north of Europe / south of Europe)

   _____

7. Which area has a larger population? (Middle East / Far East)

   _____

8. Which river is longer? (Nile River / Mississippi River)

   _____

9. Which country has a larger population? (Japan / Philippines)

   _____

10. Which is longer? (Great Wall of China / Suez Canal)

   _____

11. Which was more difficult to build? (Giza Pyramids / Buckingham Palace)

   _____

12. Which school is more famous? (University of Arizona / Princeton University)

   _____

Singular and Plural

Order the words to make logical sentences. Add *is* or *are* to each sentence. Two are questions.

1. too small / my jeans / for me

   My jeans are too small for me.

2. a long way / ten kilometers / to walk

   Ten kilometers is a long way to walk.

3. of bird / at the zoo / a new species

   There *is a new species of bird at the zoo.*

4. where / your binoculars?

   _____

5. so bad / not / my news

   _____ this time.

6. a lot of money / fifty dollars / for a book

   _____

7. a bicycle / means of transportation / only

   My _____ .

8. new or old / that TV series?

   _____

9. not / the sharp scissors / for children

   _____

10. a difficult subject / for many students / mathematics

    _____

11. than firefighters / in this city / more police

    There _____ .

Complete the sentences with combinations of the words in parentheses. Some combinations require 's or s'; some require *of*; some are noun + noun combinations. Add *the* where necessary.

1. (bag / book) I lost all my English books when my *book bag* _____
   was stolen.

2. (owner / my apartment building) *The owner of my apartment building* told me my rent
   was going up at the end of the month.

3. (children / my brother) *My brother's children* _____ are very well behaved.

4. (movie / beginning) We didn't get there in time to see _____ .

5. (back / problems) Ellen has had _____ since her accident.

6. (back / my brother) _____ has been bothering him since
   he helped us move.

7. (back / my hand) I don't know why _____ has been
   itching all day.

8. (concert / tonight) I'm really looking forward to _____ .

9. (soda / cans) Amy drank two _____ with dinner.

10. (soda / cans) Put the empty _____ into a separate plastic
    bag; we take them to a place for recycling.

11. (boat / bottom) The _____ was glass so that tourists
    could see the plants and animals in the ocean below.

12. (ocean / fish) In many countries, more _____ is eaten
    than fish from rivers and lakes.

13. (operation / two-hour) My aunt had a _____ yesterday.
    It was serious, but she's OK.

14. (this word / meaning) Can you help me with _____ ?

15. (money / problems) Stan has had _____ ever since I met him.

REVIEW

Articles and Nouns

Complete the sentences with a noun and a verb from the lists. Sometimes the noun needs -s. Use the present tense of the verb, and make it agree with the noun.

Nouns		
advice	~~bread~~	~~experience~~
furniture	hair	information
luggage	news	noise
room	room	vegetable

Verbs		
be	be	contain
~~cost~~	depress	~~form~~
help	keep	need
take	take	weigh

1. _Bread_ _costs_ more in the United States than in my country, where we buy it fresh for every meal.

2. His interesting _experiences_ traveling in China _form_ the basis of Dr. Stover's new book.

3. My doctor's _____ _____ hard to follow because I'm only allowed to eat once a day.

4. Garden _____ _____ to be more durable* than the kind used indoors.

5. Sometimes the _____ on TV _____ me because it's so negative.

6. The _____ in that hotel all _____ refrigerators and coffeemakers.

7. _____ intended for airplane travel _____ less than it did when people traveled by train.

8. _____ from the street _____ me awake some nights.

9. The _____ available on the Internet _____ people all over the world.

10. Helen's _____ _____ a long time to dry because it's so thick.

11. Most _____ _____ less time to cook than meat does.

12. I'm sorry. There _____ not _____ for all of you in my car.

* durable: *able to last a long time*

REVIEW
Articles and Nouns

Read the passage carefully. Then correct mistakes in the use of *a*, *an*, and *the*. There are fifteen mistakes; the first four are corrected.

Two of my friends and I hope we can take *a* trip to ~~the~~ southern Mexico, Belize, and Guatemala this winter. I investigated *the* cost of flights to those places, and it is pretty expensive, so I'm working with ~~the~~ *a* travel agent to find lowest price. So far, the cheapest fare has been over $900, so we're still looking for the cheaper one.

We would like to escape from a cold at home in Minnesota, visit some pyramids in area, spend some time at beach, and practice the Spanish. Of course, we'll eat new dishes and meet the new people, too. My friends think I am too interested in food, but that opinion is very unfair. In my opinion, the food in new country is just one part of culture of the country. To me, it would be a terrible mistake to go to foreign country and stay at fancy hotels and eat same food as at home.

Put a check (✔) next to the correct definition for the phrase.

1. a work day

   ✔ a. a normal working day, not a holiday

   ___ b. what you do (or are expected to do) in one day at a job

2. a day's pay

   ___ a. day on which you get paid

   ___ b. money earned for a day of work

3. a soup bowl

   ___ a. a serving of soup

   ___ b. a bowl used for soup

4. four year-old girls

   ___ a. four girls who are one year of age

   ___ b. girls who are four years of age

5. chocolate milk

   ___ a. chocolate made with milk

   ___ b. milk flavored with chocolate

6. twenty-dollar bills

   ___ a. bills that are worth $20 each

   ___ b. twenty bills that are worth $1 each

7. school girls

   ___ a. girls who are of school age

   ___ b. a school for girls only

UNIT
79

Myself/yourself/themselves, etc.

Complete the sentences. Use *-self / -selves* or *each other*. If none of the expressions are correct, write *X*.

1. I'm sure you'll be able to solve the puzzle if you concentrate __X__ hard.

2. My sister and her fiancé have been mad at _each other_ since they traveled together.

3. *A:* Who cut your hair for you?

   B: I cut it _myself_ .

4. *A:* What happened to your chin?

   B: Oh, I cut _____ while I was shaving _____ .

5. The soccer team played well and won. The girls should be proud of _____ .

6. A friend of mine and I usually meet _____ at my house before we go to play tennis.

7. I don't think Al and Laurel have known _____ long enough to get married.

8. If parents do everything for their children, the children won't learn to depend on _____ .

9. *A:* Why haven't you told anyone when you're getting married?

   B: Because my fiancé and I aren't sure of the date _____ .

10. After a short time in Canada, Maria could express _____ very well in English.

11. High school reunions give old classmates a chance to see _____ every five or ten years.

12. "Don't shoot _____ in the foot"* is good advice both to a hunter and to someone who acts in anger.

13. My grandparents take good care of _____ by eating right, exercising _____ , and sleeping enough.

14. "Class, I'll let you introduce _____ to _____ ," Mrs. Smith said to us.

15. Don't blame _____ for what happened. It wasn't your fault.

   * *A common American saying that advises people not to act in a way that is going to end up hurting them.*

A friend of mine   My own house   By myself

Complete the passage using words and phrases such as *his / his own / him / himself*.

My grandfather has lived by 1) *himself* since my grandmother died a few years ago.
We worry about 2) _____ because we think that, at eighty-two, he is too old
to live alone.

He has two children, but both live hours away, and they both have families of
3) _____ . My father and my aunt have both invited Grandpa to live with
4) _____ and 5) _____ families. But Grandpa prefers living in
6) _____ house. He says he doesn't want to leave the house, friends, and
neighbors that he has known for sixty years. Grandpa still drives and gets together
with friends of 7) _____ almost every day. We know that he can take care of
8) _____ . He shops and cooks, and he pays a teenager from the neighborhood
to clean the house every week.

My grandfather says he is doing just fine on 9) _____ . He wants us to visit
10) _____ as often as we can, though. Someone in the family goes to see him
almost every week. Sometimes I drive the two hours with a friend of 11) _____
to see how he's doing. As long as he's healthy, I think we need to respect 12) _____
decision to be on 13) _____ .

There . . . and *It . . .*

Complete the sentences, keeping the same meaning. Use *there*.

1. The box is empty.

   There is nothing OR _There isn't anything_____ in the box.

2. This small town has no high school.

   There _____ in this small town.

3. You can drive as fast as you want on this road.

   _____ no speed limit _____ .

4. No one came to the airport to meet me.

   _____ no one to meet me at _____ .

5. My coffee is very sweet.

   _____ sugar in _____ .

6. We didn't eat because we were in a hurry.

   We _____ because _____ enough time.

7. We might have a party next week.

   _____ at our place _____ .

8. There isn't a stop sign at that corner anymore.

   _____ used to _____ .

9. I can't work here with all the noise.

   _____ too much _____ for me to _____ .

There . . . and *It . . .*

Complete B's answers. Use the words in parentheses and *there* or *it* + a present or past form of *be*. Some sentences are negative.

A.	**B.**
1. Was the storm bad?	(terrible) Yes. *It was terrible.*
2. Was the storm bad?	(a lot of damage) Yes. *There was a lot of damage.*
3. Why don't we drive to New Orleans this weekend?	(too far) No. _____ Let's fly instead.
4. Can I have some cream in my coffee?	(any cream) Sorry, _____ .
5. Did you go on a hike last weekend?	(nice enough) No. _____ to go hiking. We stayed home.
6. Can I borrow your camera for the weekend?	(something wrong with it) Sorry. _____
7. Have you heard the news about Rosa?	(wonderful) Yes, I have. _____ that she's getting married.
8. It's a little late, but do you want to stop and see Kevin?	(a light) Why don't we? _____ on in the living room.
9. Amy said to stop by* anytime. Do you want to stop by now?	(too late to stop by) I don't think so. _____ without calling first.
10. Should we serve apple pie to our guests for dessert?	(enough for everyone) We can't. _____
11. Did you like the Turkish film you saw?	(very interesting) Yes, I did. _____
12. Are you going to get a flu shot* this year?	(a lot of flu at work last year) Yes, I think I will. _____
13. How is the weather in Moscow?	(a lot of snow there last winter) Cold, I think. _____

* stop by: *to visit for a short time*
* flu shot: *a vaccination against influenza*

Some and *any*

Complete the passage with *some* or *any*, or with *some-* / *any-* + *body/thing/where*.

1) _Something_ strange happened the other day at the supermarket. I was buying

2) _some_ groceries when 3) _____ started talking to me.

He asked, "How's it going, Mike?" My name isn't Mike, and I didn't recognize the man,

so I was confused. I tried to place his face, but I couldn't think of 4) _____

that I might have met him. He just went on talking, and I kept trying to think of

5) _____ to say. Finally, I told him that I was not his friend Mike and that I

didn't even know 6) _____ called Mike. Now *he* was confused. Obviously, I

looked like 7) _____ that he knew. Finally, he said, "I'm sorry. I didn't mean to

cause 8) _____ trouble. You look just like 9) _____ that I

used to work with at Acme Computers."

The strange part of all this is that I have worked at Acme Computers for five years! But I knew I

didn't know the man *or* "Mike." "That's all right," I said. " 10) _____ can

make a mistake." I thought it would be better not to say 11) _____ about

working at Acme, though. Strange world!

NIT
83

No/none/any *Nothing/nobody*, etc.

Answer the questions two ways: (a) with a short answer using *none, no one,*
nothing, **or** *nowhere;* **and (b) with a full sentence using** *not + any, anyone,*
anything, **or** *anywhere.*

1. How many eggs did you break? *None* . I *didn't break any eggs* .

2. What are you doing tonight? *Nothing* . I _____
_____ tonight.

3. Who did you tell about my speeding ticket? _____ .
I _____ .

4. Where are the Smiths going on vacation this year? _____ .
They _____ .

5. How much money do I owe you? _____ .
You _____ .

6. What did Fred say about me? _____ .
He _____ you.

7. Where would you like to go tomorrow? _____ .
I _____ .

8. How much free time does Rob have? _____ .
He _____ .

9. Who did you give money to? _____ .
I _____ .

10. How many people did you invite to the party? _____ .
We _____ .

11. Who did you invite to the party? _____ .
We _____ .

No/none/any   *Nothing/nobody*, etc.

Read what a mother is saying to her sixteen-year-old son about his responsibilities at home. Then complete the passage with *no*, *any*, or *none*.

"Don't tell me you have **1)** _no_ time to help out at home. I don't care if

2) _____ of your friends have to do chores* around the house. Maybe your

friends don't have parents who both work. But that doesn't make **3)** _____

difference. **4)** _____ child should grow up without helping the family.

We give you an allowance* to teach you to handle* money. You can spend it in

5) _____ way that you want. We give you chores to do to teach you

responsibility. **6)** _____ of the chores are very hard or take much time.

There will be **7)** _____ excuses for not doing your chores. Is that

absolutely clear?"

"Yes, Mom."

* chores: *routine work at home such as making beds and cutting the grass*
* allowance: *money that parents give children regularly*
* handle: *to deal with, manage, control*

Much, many, little, few, a lot, plenty

Find the mistakes and correct them. If there are no mistakes, write *right*.

1. Diane comes from a small family. She has very little relatives.

   She has very few relatives.

2. I don't know many people who live alone.

   Right

3. My brother spends much time fixing his car.

   _____

4. We won't have trouble finding a place to stay in Los Angeles. There are plenty hotels there.

   _____

5. Martha is a lucky woman. She has a few enemies.

   _____

6. I have very little money on me, so I can't treat you to lunch today. Sorry.

   _____

7. Josh has lots clothes. Why does he need to borrow yours?

   _____

8. My grandparents are very active. They go out much.

   _____

9. Mr. James isn't a very good boss. He has a little patience.

   _____

10. It cost very little to fix my car. Was I lucky!

    _____

11. There aren't much reasons to visit that town unless you like old mines.

    _____

12. I ate few hours ago, but I'm hungry again.

    _____

EXERCISE 108

UNITS
85-86 *All / all of, most / most of, no / none of, etc.*
Both / both of, neither / neither of, either / either of

Complete the sentences using the words in parentheses. Sometimes you need to add *the*, *of*, or *of the*.

1. (most / people) We invited _most of the people_ that we know to our daughter's wedding.

2. (neither / answer) Ben solved the math problem two different ways, but _neither answer_ was right.

3. Jake's grandfather is not very well. (most / days) He spends _____ in bed.

4. (both / presents) Julia couldn't decide whether to get her sister a bracelet or a camera, so she got _____ .

5. (both / them) Ken and Sarah wanted to go to the concert with us, but there weren't enough tickets for _____ .

6. (either / his brothers) Joe doesn't talk to _____ very often.

7. (either / author) Mark recommended two books to me, but I had never heard of
_____ .

8. We went to Los Angeles for the weekend. (both / days) We spent _____
with friends who live there.

9. (some / days) _____ the weather here is beautiful, but other days it's very gray.

10. (neither / presents) _____ cost a lot, but Jeremy was very pleased with both of them.

11. (some / money) I lent Brenda _____ . (a few / dollars) However, I had
to keep _____ for myself for tomorrow.

12. (neither / city) Prague and Ljiubiana have beautiful old buildings to visit because
_____ was bombed during World War II.

13. (neither / them) Both Claudia and her sister want to visit Poland next summer, but
_____ has saved any money.

All / all of, most / most of, no / none of, etc.
Both / both of, neither / neither of, either / either of

Complete the descriptions of the picture. Use *all (of)*, *none (of)*, *both (of)*, *neither (of)*, or *either (of)*.

1. ___*All*___ the basketball players are wearing uniforms.

2. ___*None of*___ them are playing basketball in street clothes.

3. _____ the girls has short hair.

4. _____ the boys have short hair.

5. _____ the girls is taller than the boys.

6. The girl with the ball doesn't want _____ the boys to get it.

7. _____ the players is an adult.

8. _____ team has five players.

9. _____ the girls is wearing a sweatband, but _____ the boys are.

10. _____ these teenagers are wearing athletic shoes.

11. _____ the players are sitting down and relaxing.

12. It seems that _____ the players are having fun.

All, every, and whole
Each and every

Complete the passage. Use *all*, *each*, *every*, *everyone*, or *whole*.

My friend Rob is a good friend, but he can be inflexible* sometimes. I mean, he has to have
things his own way* or he's not happy. For example, Rob takes a two-week vacation from the
bank **1)** _every_ August. His wife and children always want to go away somewhere,
but Rob insists on spending **2)** _all_ his vacations working in the yard at home.
Last year he spent the **3)** _____ two weeks of vacation working in his vegetable
garden. **4)** _____ else in the family wanted to go to Vancouver, but Rob would
not go. Since he did not want to go, the **5)** _____ family had to miss a nice vacation.

6) _____ month, Rob, some other friends, and I meet to play golf, have dinner,
or do something else together. When a lot of people go out to dinner together, it's usually
easier to split the bill*: **7)** _____ person pays an equal share. But Rob never agrees
to split the bill – he insists on paying for exactly what he ordered, no more and no less.
This can be embarrassing for **8)** _____ else in the group. We have to sit there
waiting while Rob takes out his calculator to figure out *his* bill. **9)** _____ of us
were really upset with Rob the last time this happened because the waiter became
very impatient with us.

Some of us have talked to Rob about his inflexibility, but he doesn't see what the problem is.
He thinks his behavior is normal and fair to everyone. I guess we will just have to accept him
the way he is. That's **10)** _____ we can do.

* inflexible: *unwilling to change your way of doing things*
* have things (one's) own way: *to have what you want*
* split the bill: *to divide the cost and share equally*

Use your own ideas to write new sentences with the underlined words.

1. I have a <u>lot of</u> patience, but I don't have <u>much</u> tolerance for stingy* people.

   My friends have a lot of time but not much money.

   Many people get very bad headaches, but doctors can't give much help.

2. I've been invited to <u>two</u> parties this weekend, but I don't want to go to <u>either of them</u>.

   My sister borrowed two books from the library and said I could read either of them.

   Two salespeople called me last night, but I didn't talk to either of them.

3. I like <u>most</u> people, but I don't have <u>many</u> close friends.

4. I have <u>very few</u> problems with my computer now. I had <u>a little</u> trouble in the beginning, though.

5. <u>Most of my friends</u> are married, and about <u>half of them</u> have children.

6. A coworker didn't invite <u>any of</u> his friends to his wedding, and <u>none of them</u> gave him a present.

7. My parents <u>both</u> work, and <u>neither of them</u> wants to retire*.

8. <u>No one</u> in my family is a lawyer or a doctor, but <u>some</u> are accountants.

9. My uncle has <u>plenty of</u> money, but he never gives <u>any</u> to <u>anyone</u>.

   * stingy: *spending or giving unwillingly*
   * retire: *to stop working, often because of reaching a particular age, such as sixty-five*

Relative Clauses – Clauses with *who/that/which*
Relative Clauses – Clauses with or without *who/that/which*

Relative Clauses

Complete the sentences with relative clauses. Form the clauses from the sentences in the box. Use *who*, *which*, and *that* only when necessary. Include any necessary prepositions.

> a. The family used to live next door.
> b. The teacher gave him a lot of help after class.
> ✔ c. You were talking about a wedding.
> d. He liked her the best.
> ✔ e. Kate recommended the movie.
> f. You went to school with those people.
> g. You're pointing to a man.
> h. I can depend on the friend in an emergency.
> i. We met a Mexican couple on vacation.
> j. I like the music.
> k. I left money for you on the table.
> ✔ l. It is known for its views and hilly streets.

1. San Francisco is a pretty city _that is known for its views and hilly streets_ .
   (*that* = subject)

2. Are we going to see the movie _Kate recommended_ ?

3. Did you go to the wedding _you were talking about_ ?

4. I need a friend _____ .

5. Did you get the money _____ ?

6. Roger bought a thank-you card for a teacher _____ .

7. Roger also bought a present for the classmate _____ .

8. We wrote to the Mexican couple _____ .

9. I don't see the man _____ .

10. My children don't like the kind of music _____ .

11. Do you still see the people _____ ?

12. I have no idea what happened to the family _____ .

Relative Clauses – Clauses with *who/that/which*
Relative Clauses – Clauses with or without *who/that/which*

Put parentheses around *who*, *which*, or *that* when they are optional.

1. Is this the box (that) you were looking for? – (*that* is optional)

2. Is this the box that was in the garage? – (*that* is necessary)

3. Do you know the name of the song which we just listened to?

4. Did you call the man who wanted to talk to you?

5. Did you call the woman who you wanted to talk to?

6. Sylvia hasn't seen the people that she used to work with for years.

7. Have you eaten all the food that was in the fridge?

8. Have you eaten all the food that we bought together?

9. Mary Lou said something that hurt my feelings.

10. Mary Lou said something that was both unkind and untrue.

11. Did you see anyone that we know at the party?

12. Did Helen see the movie that was recommended so highly?

13. My brother hates the movie star that I was just watching on TV.

14. "People who live in glass houses shouldn't throw stones."*

15. The people who you live with are very nice.

  * *This proverb advises us not to judge or criticize others because they can easily do the same to us. We are all open to criticism.*

Relative Clauses – *whose/whom/where*

Complete the sentences below using relative clauses with *who, whose, whom, where, that,* or *why*. Form the relative clauses from what the people say.

✔1. My father is very rich.

1. My brother is engaged to a woman <u>whose father is very rich</u>.

✔2. I'm afraid of heights.

2. I know a firefighter <u>who is afraid of heights</u>.

✔3. We stayed there on our honeymoon.

3. The couple showed us pictures of the hotel ____ <u>where they stayed on their honeymoon</u>.

✔4. I have fallen in love with her.

4. The woman with <u>whom he has fallen in love</u> _____ is older than him.

5. My wife wants a bigger house.

5. His wife has never told him the reason _____ _____ _____ .

6. We got married today.

6. I met a nice young couple on the day _____ _____ _____ .

EXERCISE CONTINUES ▶ ▶

7. I want to be a soccer player when I grow up.

7. I enjoyed talking to the girl _____ _____ _____ .

8. My wife and my daughter are both police officers.

8. The man _____ _____ _____ seemed very proud.

9. I am moving to a new apartment.

Sheila

9. I forget the reason _____ Sheila _____ _____ .

10. People get passports here.

10. The two women went downtown to the building _____ _____ .

11. I sold my car to him.

11. The man to _____ he _____ _____ doesn't have it anymore.

12. We went to Alaska this year.

12. They can't afford to go to Mexico in the same year _____ _____ .

Relative Clauses – "Extra Information" Clauses

Write sentences with extra information relative clauses. Make the clauses from the sentences in the box. Use *which, whose,* **or** *many of / most of whom.*

 1. camel

 2. dolphin

 3. donkey

 4. eagle

 5. elephant

 6. goat

 7. kangaroo

 8. llama

 9. ostrich

 10. rattlesnake

 11. shark

a. This is surprising because they are intelligent, friendly animals.
b. It is an animal in the horse family with short legs and long ears.
c. They are known to travel long distances without water.
d. Their tusks are made into ivory jewelry and decorations.
e. A pouch is like a big pocket made of skin.
f. Most of them haven't seen a dangerous animal.
✔g. They are actually sea animals rather than fish.
h. Its wool is soft and expensive.
i. It can't fly.
j. They have sharp beaks and very good sight.
k. They have a reputation* for eating anything.
l. Many of them hunt illegally.

1. Dolphins often jump above the surface of the water.

   Dolphins, which are actually sea animals rather than fish, often jump above the
   surface of the water.

   * reputation: *the opinion that people in general have about someone/something*

   EXERCISE CONTINUES ▶ ▶

2. The ostrich can run very fast.

_____

3. Eagles hunt and eat small animals.·

_____

4. Americans sometimes compare a foolish or stubborn* person to a donkey.

_____

5. I have always been fascinated* by camels.

_____

6. Elephants are protected in many countries.

_____

7. Elephants are once again being killed by hunters.

_____

8. The kangaroo carries its young in its pouch.

_____

9. Goats live wild in mountain areas or are kept on farms.

_____

10. Many people are afraid of animals like rattlesnakes and sharks.

_____

11. The llama is at home in the Andes Mountains of South America.

_____

12. Some swimmers are afraid of dolphins.

_____

* stubborn: *opposed to changing your opinion*
* fascinated (by): *interested (in)*

-ing and -ed Phrases (*the woman talking to Tom, the boy injured in the accident*)

A. Answer the questions. Find the answer in the box. Write it as an *–ing* or *–ed* phrase with the appropriate noun.

> a. The ones who hope to get scholarships*
> b. The one which offered more benefits*
> ✔c. The one that goes up the mountain
> d. The ones who are employed at the mine
> e. The ones who were confused by the homework
> f. The one which employs 250 workers
> g. The one who was interviewed last week
> ✔h. The ones that are made by famous designers

1. Which trail* did you take?   *The trail going up the mountain*
2. Which clothes cost more?   *The clothes made by famous designers*
3. Which students need to get good grades?   The students _____
_____
4. Which person got the job?   The secretary _____
5. Which company is going to close?   _____
6. Which workers went on strike?   _____
7. Which job did Gloria take?   _____
8. Which students needed to talk to the teacher?   _____

B. Write complete sentences to answer questions 1 to 6.

1. *I took the trail going up the mountain.*

2. *The clothes made by famous designers cost more.*

3. The students _____ grades.

4. The secretary _____ .

5. The radio company _____ .

6. _____

* scholarship: *money given to somebody to pay for their education*
* benefits: *extras like health insurance, a paid vacation, etc., which a company gives employees*
* trail: *a path for hiking*

Relative Clauses

Use your own ideas to complete the sentences.

1. I would like to meet someone that _has been in the United Arab Emirates_ .
   I would like to meet someone that _____ .

2. I would like to have met _Indira Gandhi_ , who _was prime minister of India_ .
   I would like to have met _____ , who _____ .

3. I would like to meet _____ , who _____ .

4. _____ a person whose _____ .

5. _____ someone I _____ .

6. _____ something I _____ .

7. People who _____ usually have a lot of _____ .

8. A friend _____ , which _____ .

9. _____ , with whom _____ .

10. One day _____ , where _____ .

11. _____ a place where _____ .

12. _____ two _____ , both of whom _____ .

13. _____ two _____ , neither of which _____ .

14. _____ the day that _____ .

Adjectives Ending in *-ing* and *-ed* (*boring/bored*, etc.)

Complete B's answers. Use a form of *be* (*is, are, was, will be*, etc.) and an *-ing* or *-ed* adjective made from the verb in parentheses.

A	B

A

1. How did you like the film?

2. Why doesn't the cat want to go outside?

3. What does your brother think of the political scandal?

4. How was your doctor's appointment?

5. What did you think of the movie?

6. Is Monica going to the movies with us tonight?

7. Did you enjoy your vacation?

8. Do you understand the directions on this bottle?

9. When are your parents leaving for China?

10. Did you like the play last night?

11. How was your job interview?

12. How will the weather be while we are in Quebec?

13. Were there a lot of people at the party?

B

1. (interest) It _was interesting_ .

2. (frighten) It _'s frightened_ .

3. (disgust) He _____ . He expects more of politicians.

4. (depress) It _____ . The doctor said my health was very poor.

5. (upset) It _____ _____ because of all the violence.

6. (interest) No, I don't think she _____ _____ in going.

7. (disappoint) No, we _____ very _____ . The weather was terrible.

8. (confuse) No, I don't. I think they _____ a little _____ .

9. (excite) Next week. They _____ _____ about going.

10. (amuse) Yes, it _____ .

11. (embarrass) I _____ because I answered the questions badly.

12. (freeze) I think it _____ . Make sure you pack warm clothes.

13. (surprise) Yes, there really _____ a _____ number of people there.

Adjectives: Word Order (*a nice new house*)   Adjectives after Verbs (*You look tired*)

Complete the answers. Use the adjectives in parentheses plus any other necessary words.

1. What kind of sweater would you like?
   (green / large / woolen) I'd like _a large green woolen_ _____ one.

2. What kind of house did Gary and Paula buy?
   (old / big / beautiful / stone) They bought a _____ house.

3. What is your nephew like?
   (sixteen-year-old / typical / city) He _____
   _____ boy.

4. What kind of car does your uncle have?
   (blue / German / big / old) He _____ car.

5. What does your lost cat look like?
   (cute / brown / grey) It's _____ kitten.

6. What kind of music do your parents listen to?
   (Mexican / favorite / traditional) They listen to their _____
   _____ music.

7. What shall we eat tonight?
   (new / Thai / great) Let's go to that _____ restaurant.

8. What did Susan spend her money on?
   (old / gorgeous / Central Asian) She _____
   _____ jewelry.

9. What kind of friends does Mike have?
   (nice / foreign / young) He has a lot of _____ friends.

10. What kind of furniture did the couple buy?
    (black / white / steel / modern) They _____
    _____ furniture.

Complete the sentences, keeping the same meaning.

1. Cindy's paintings are beautiful.

   Cindy paints *beautifully* .

2. Don doesn't drive very safely.

   Don isn't a *very safe* driver.

3. Mark is an incredibly quick typist.

   Mark types .

4. Marcia speaks French really fluently.

   Marcia is in French.

5. Julia is a very slow worker.

   Julia works .

6. Paul is talking very strangely for some reason.

   Paul's voice sounds .

7. Mrs. Grey gave the dress a careful look before buying it.

   Mrs. Grey looked at .

8. We have had continuous rain for three days.

   It has rained .

9. Jim was injured in the accident, but the injury wasn't serious.

   Jim wasn't .

10. Pat made a surprisingly quick recovery from her accident.

    Pat recovered .

11. My boss answered my question coldly and briefly, I'd say.

    My boss's answer sounded to me.

12. It seems to me that the situation is very serious.

    looks to me.

Adjectives and Adverbs (*well/fast/late, hard/hardly*)

Complete the passage with *fast, hard, hardly, late, lately, good,* or *well*.

Things have changed around the office where I work. We are all trying very **1)** _hard_
to please the boss, Mr. Brown. He has been in a bad mood* **2)** _lately_ , and, of course
we want to stay on his good side*. Maybe he doesn't feel **3)** _good_ OR _well_ , or maybe
something happened that we don't know about. Anyway, nobody in the office gets to work
4) _late_ anymore. We stay at work **5)** _____ if necessary, we work
6) _____ , and we treat the customers **7)** _____ . We take only half an hour
for lunch, so we have to eat very **8)** _____ . We **9)** _____ have time to eat
a sandwich.

I am not sure what is bothering Mr. Brown, but I hope he gets over* it **10)** _____ .
All the workers like him because he has always treated us **11)** _____ . He
12) _____ ever gets angry. We work a long day, but we are paid **13)** _____ .
We all hope that Mr. Brown returns to his normal **14)** _____ mood soon.

* in a bad mood: *unhappy, angry*.
* stay on someone's good side: *not to do anything to annoy the person*
* get over (something): *to return to your normal state (of health, happiness, etc.)*

So and *such*

A. Complete B's answers. Use the words in parentheses and *so* or *such*. Use an appropriate tense.

A	**B**
1. Why did Sam forget his keys?	(be / in a hurry) Because _he was in such a hurry_ .
2. Why did Sam forget his keys?	(be / nervous) Because _he was so nervous_ .
3. Why don't you want to go out to eat tonight?	(have / much food at home) Because we _____ _____ .
4. Why is Amy going to stay home from work tomorrow?	(have / a bad cold) Because she _____ .
5. Why didn't you walk to work this morning?	(be / cold) Because it _____ .
6. Why didn't you say goodbye to Kevin last night?	(be / busy) Because he _____ .
7. (*at a party*) It's late. Why don't you want to go home?	(have / a good time) Because I _____ _____ .
8. Why are you skipping* lunch today?	(have / a big breakfast) Because I _____ _____ .

B. Rewrite the responses above with *so . . . that* and *such . . . that* so that they are complete sentences.

1. _Sam was in such a hurry that he forgot his keys._

2. _Sam was so nervous that he forgot his keys._

3. We have _____ .

4. Amy has _____ .

5. It _____ .

6. Kevin was _____ .

7. I am _____ .

8. I had _____ .

* skip (something): *not to have or do something*

Enough and too

A. Order the words in parentheses to make sentences. Two are questions.

1. (too / speech / notes / take / to / was / on / disorganized / his)

   His speech was too disorganized to take notes on.

2. (isn't / enough / Mrs. / to live by herself / healthy / Garcia)

   _____

3. (to wear / was / for Millie / jacket / too / the / small)

   _____

4. (enough / isn't / car / Josh / drive / a / to / old)

   _____

5. (nice / such a terrible thing / do / is / George / too / to)

   _____

6. (enough / you / do / to lend me some? / have / money)

   _____

7. (on time / enough / this / fast / type / report / I / to finish / can't)

   _____

8. (water / is / enough / life / on Mars? / to support / there)

   _____

B. Rewrite sentences 2 to 5. Use too instead of enough, or enough instead of too. Substitute the words in parentheses, and make any other necessary changes.

1. (organized) _His speech was not organized enough to take notes on._

2. (sick) _____ too sick _____ .

3. (big) _____

4. (young) _____

5. (mean) _____

EXERCISE 124

Comparison – *cheaper, more expensive*, etc.

Complete the sentences using the comparative form of the adjectives and adverbs in the box.

bad	calm	carefully	cheap	early	easy
friendly	hard	interesting	large	loudly	modern
safe	slowly	thin	well		

1. You're driving too fast. Could you please drive _more slowly_ ?

2. Kim is too nervous to talk now. Wait till she's a little _calmer_ .

3. This house is too old fashioned. I'd like to live in a house that's _____ .

4. These shirts are pretty expensive. Don't you have any that are _____ ?

5. Glen's sick today. Let's not visit him until he's feeling _____ .

6. I'm a little heavy now. I'll be able to wear these pants when I'm _____ .

7. This Arabic book is too hard for me. Do you have one that is _____ ?

8. I find watching TV boring. Can't we do something _____ ?

9. We stayed up too late last night. Tonight we're going to bed _____ .

10. This rental car* is too small for four people. Let's get one that's _____ .

11. We can't hear you in the back of the room. Please speak _____ .

12. Our teacher is too easy on us. I'd like a teacher who is _____ .

13. This road looks a little dangerous to me. Can't we take one that's _____ ?

14. I think my mechanic is a little careless. I'm going to look for one who does his work

    _____ .

15. My doctor's good, but he's pretty unfriendly. I'd like a doctor who's _____ .

16. I won't go to the doctor unless my headache gets _____ .

    * rental car: *a car rented from a company for a day, a week, etc.*

Comparison

Complete the conversations. Use one word in each blank.

1. A: Does Melanie miss work very often?

   B: She doesn't miss work __any__ more often than other people. Why?

   A: I'm upset with people who miss work. The __more__ people miss work, the _____ work the rest of us have to do.

   B: That's true. But when you missed work for a month, we did your work for you. Remember?

   A: Yes, I guess I need to be _____ more understanding.

   B: That's all right. _____ longer you work here, the _____ you'll understand things.

2. A: I've been playing tennis for two years, but I don't seem to get _____ better.

   B: That's not true. You're getting better and _____ all the time.

   A: Are you sure? To me, it seems like the _____ I practice, the worse I play.

   B: Not at all. It's just that* I practice a lot _____ than you, so my game is improving a little _____ than yours.

   A: I see. The _____ I think about it, _____ more it seems you're right. Thanks.

3. A: Aren't you ready yet?

   B: No. The less you talk to me, _____ _____ I will be ready.

   A: Sorry. It's just that we're late. And the _____ we arrive at the movies, the _____ seats we'll get.

   B: You're right, but I can't get ready any _____ . I won't take _____ longer, I promise.

   * It is just that . . . : *The reason for that is . . .*

Comparison – *cheaper, more expensive*, etc.
Comparison – *as . . . as / than*

Complete the sentences, keeping the same meaning.

1. My sister isn't as tall as I am.
   I'm *taller than my sister*   .

2. They didn't have as much fun as we did.
   We *had more fun than they did*   .

3. I eat less fish than I used to.
   I don't _____ as I used to.

4. I don't have as much free time as you do.
   You have _____ than I do.

5. Paul feels worse today than yesterday.
   He doesn't _____ as yesterday.

6. Jack talks less than his brother.
   Jack doesn't _____ his brother.

7. I don't drive as far to work as Kate does.
   Kate _____ I do.

8. Sarah isn't as friendly as she used to be.
   Sarah used _____ .

9. Martin answered the question less intelligently than I expected.
   Martin didn't _____ .

10. There were fewer people at the game than usual.
    There weren't _____ .

11. Barbara is sadder than she seems.
    Barbara isn't _____ .

12. These shoes aren't as uncomfortable as they look.
    These shoes are _____ .

Superlatives – *the longest / the most enjoyable*, etc.

**Complete the conversations with the superlative. Use the words in parentheses,
in or *of* if needed, and any other necessary words.**

1. *A:* Is Brazil a big country?

   B: (big country / South America) Yes, it's _the biggest country in South America_ .

2. *A:* I hear that you had a bad storm in Florida.

   B: (serious storm / the year) Yes, it was _the most serious storm of the year_ .

3. *A:* Pat is pretty busy, isn't she?

   B: (busy people) Yes, she's one _____ that I know.

4. *A:* This is wonderful coffee.

   B: (good coffee) Yes, it's _____ I've ever tasted.

5. *A:* How old is Mark?

   B: (old child / his family) I'm not sure, but he's _____ .

6. *A:* Is Brussels an expensive city?

   B: (expensive cities / Europe) Yes, it's one _____ .

7. *A:* Did your friends stay at a nice hotel?

   B: (nice hotel / the city) Yes, they stayed at _____ .

8. *A:* (famous person) Who is _____ you've ever met?

   B: Let me think. The governor, I guess.

9. *A:* Is spring a pleasant season in Chile?

   B: (pleasant season / the year) Yes, I think it's _____ .

10. *A:* Is your local football team good?

    B: (good teams / the country) Yes, it's one _____ .

11. *A:* Which is safer, a train or a bus?

    B: (safe form of transportation) Actually, I think the airplane is _____

    _____ that you can take.

UNITS
105-
106

Word Order – Verb + Object; Place and Time
Word Order – Adverbs with the Verb

Complete the sentences with the words given. Put the words in the correct order.

1. usually / for breakfast / during the week / don't / time / have

   I *don't usually have time for breakfast during the week* .

2. his lunch / again / burned / probably / has

   Pablo _____ .

3. forgot / almost / last week / your birthday

   I _____ .

4. walk / a cane / Lee / can / only / with

   Mr. _____ .

5. in the winter / Mrs. Conrad / abroad / usually / travel / don't

   Mr. and _____ .

6. hot chocolate / every morning / at her desk / likes to drink

   Mona _____ .

7. on the weekends / has / never / go hiking / time to

   Hannah _____ .

8. suit / new / a lot / like / your / and overcoat

   I _____ .

9. seldom / on Saturday / in her apartment / is

   Sarah _____ .

10. your glasses / forgot / last night / at my house

    You _____ .

11. definitely / on time / to work / will / get / next week

    I _____ .

12. sings with / on the weekend / in a choir / his friends / also

    Ken _____ .

Still, *yet*, and *already*   *Anymore / any longer / no longer*

**Look at the pictures of a street in a small town ten years ago and today.
Read the sentences about ten years ago. Complete the sentences about today
with *still* or *not . . . anymore*.**

Main Street ten years ago

Main Street today

1. There used to be a hotel on Main Street ten years ago.

   There *isn't a hotel on Main Street*

   anymore   .

2. There was a hardware store on Main Street.

   There *is still a hardware store there*

   _____ .

3. There was a dry cleaner's.

   There _____

   _____ .

4. There were lots of cars on Main Street before.

   There _____

   _____ .

5. Teenagers used to ride their bikes on Main Street.

   Teenagers _____

   _____ .

6. We used to be able to go to the movies on Main Street.

   We _____

   _____ .

7. People had trouble parking downtown before.

   People _____

   _____ .

8. You could find something to read in town in the old days.

   You _____

   _____ .

Still, *yet*, and *already*   *Anymore* / *any longer* / *no longer*

Put *still*, *yet*, *already*, or *anymore* in the underlined group of words.

1. Joe got divorced two years ago, and he's~~ ~~single.
   still

2. I used to ride my bike to work, but I don't ride it to work~~ ~~.
   anymore

3. I can't go out yet. I'm waiting for my brother to call. I have been waiting for his call all afternoon.

4. I'm waiting for your answer. You haven't said anything.

5. I was going to tell Elaine the bad news, but she knew about your accident.

6. Michael used to be very athletic. He jogs pretty often.

7. Julia always makes decisions at the last minute. Has she decided if she is coming to dinner with us?

8. I used to eat at that Korean restaurant a lot. I don't eat there.

9. (*on the phone*) A: Are we going out to eat tonight?
   B: No, I've started cooking dinner.

10. A: Do you want to drive up to Montreal on the weekend?
    B: Yes. Why? Have you changed your mind again?

11. I want to change jobs, but I'm not ready to do it.

12. A: Should we buy Helen a microwave oven as a wedding present?
    B: No, she has one.

13. Mark has gained weight. His clothes don't fit him.

14. A: Are you ready to leave?
    B: No, I have a few things to do.

15. A: Do you go hiking on the weekends like before?
    B: No, we don't have time.

Even

Complete the passage with *even*, *even if*, or *even though*.

A friend, Sylvia, used to have insomnia*. She is thirty-seven, a bank teller, and married with two children. She couldn't fall asleep at night **1)** *even though* she worked hard every day and felt tired at night. She tried different solutions to cure her insomnia. She tried exercising before bedtime, but it was **2)** _____ harder to fall asleep after exercising. Then she tried sleeping pills **3)** _____ she doesn't like to take pills. They helped her fall asleep, but she felt tired the next day. Someone advised her to take a hot bath before going to bed. Unfortunately, that made her feel **4)** _____ less sleepy at bedtime.

I suspect* Sylvia was one of those people who can't relax when the day is over. **5)** _____ her body was tired at the end of the day, her mind was very active. She worried a lot – about work, her family, the house, **6)** _____ the cat and dog. Sometimes she worried about people that she didn't **7)** _____ know!

When I saw her last week, Sylvia was doing wonderfully, though. She was worrying less and sleeping much better. Before, she worried about everything. Now, somehow she realizes that worrying doesn't help things. "Whatever is going to happen will happen. I can't change it," she said to me. Now, **8)** _____ the telephone rings in the middle of the night, it doesn't wake her up. She sleeps very soundly* the whole night. Some nights, she **9)** _____ goes to bed before her children do.

I am going to ask Sylvia how she solved her problem. I would like to know how she learned to worry less **10)** _____ I don't have trouble sleeping.

* insomnia: *inability to sleep*
* suspect: *to have an idea; to believe*
* soundly: *deeply, well*

Adjectives and Adverbs

Use your own ideas to write one sentence with all three of the words in parentheses.

1. (hard / well / quickly)

   If I study hard, I'll learn quickly and be able to speak English well soon.

   I work hard but not very quickly; my work is always well done, though.

   _____

2. (boring / long / perfectly) _____

   _____

3. (South American / unusual / incredibly) _____

   _____

4. (quietly / dead / black) _____

   _____

5. (interested / silver / hardly) _____

   _____

6. (happily / disappointing / lately) _____

   _____

7. (fast / surprisingly / late) _____

   _____

8. (satisfied / sadly / lonely) _____

   _____

Adjectives and Adverbs

Rewrite the sentences so that they make sense. Use the correct form of a new adjective or adverb to replace the underlined word(s).

1. I enjoy being with Jean because she's one of the <u>saddest</u> people I know.

   I enjoy being with Jean because she's one of the happiest people I know.

2. I like eating at my aunt's because she's a <u>worse</u> cook than me.

   I like eating at my aunt's because she's a better cook than me.

3. It takes Kevin longer to get home because he doesn't live as <u>far from</u> work as I do.

4. I'm staying home from school because my cold is <u>better</u> today than it was yesterday.

5. Sam bought the beige rug because it didn't cost as <u>little</u> as the blue one.

6. Everyone would like to be married to the <u>meanest</u> person in the world.

7. A friend of mine lost his job because he wasn't as <u>lazy</u> as his coworkers.

8. New technology is making cars <u>more and more dangerous</u>.

9. Coffee and tea are among the <u>most expensive</u> beverages* in the world.

10. As time goes by, computers are becoming <u>more expensive</u> and <u>less</u> common.

11. Fred can wear my clothes because he's <u>a different</u> size <u>from</u> me.

   * beverage: *a drink*

EXERCISE 134

UNITS
101-
104

REVIEW
Adjectives and Adverbs

Complete the conversations. Use the words in parentheses in the correct form and any other necessary words.

1. *A:* Is the food in that restaurant good?

   B: (good restaurant) Yes, a lot of people think it's <u> *the best restaurant in* </u> town.

2. *A:* Why aren't you going to Hawaii with your friends?

   B: (much money) I don't have <u> *as much money as* </u> they do.

3. *A:* Why are you so tired tonight? It's not very late.

   B: (early) I probably got up <u> *earlier than* </u> you today.

4. *A:* (rich person) Who is _____ the world?
   B: I'm not sure. It might be Bill Gates.

5. *A:* How is your dad doing after his accident?

   B: (badly) He's not doing _____ I thought. He can walk normally.

6. *A:* Why did David get a raise? I didn't get one.

   B: (hard) Maybe he works _____ you.

7. *A:* Are you finished eating? Ready for dessert?

   B: (slowly) No, I eat _____ you.

8. *A:* (big) Which country has a _____ population, China or India?

   B: (populous country) Right now, China is _____ the world.

9. *A:* Would it be better to go to Thailand in the spring or the summer?

   B: (nice) In my opinion, summer isn't _____ spring there.

10. *A:* (easy) This computer game is hard. Don't you have an _____ one?

    B: (easy) No, that is _____ one that I have.

11. *A:* (badly) Sheryl did _____ me on the test.

    B: (much) Maybe she didn't study _____ you.

12. *A:* (often) Ted doesn't come to see us _____ he used to.

    B: (busy) No, his job keeps him a lot _____ before.

REVIEW

Adjectives and Adverbs

Use your own ideas to write new sentences with the underlined words.

1. I don't <u>have as much</u> free time as I used to.

   My brother doesn't have as much patience as me.

   Many people don't have as much money as they need.

   _____

2. <u>The</u> colder it gets, <u>the happier</u> my friend Pat is. She hates the heat.

   The better my English gets, the happier I am.

   The longer my parents are married, the happier they seem together.

   _____

3. My best friend <u>isn't as</u> smart as me, <u>but</u> she is more successful.

   Driving isn't as expensive as flying, but it takes longer.

   _____

4. <u>The more</u> my uncle worries about his job, the thinner he gets.

   _____

5. My cousin told us <u>the</u> strangest story <u>I've ever</u> heard in my life.

   _____

6. <u>The happiest day of my life</u> was when I got married.

   _____

7. My friend's coworkers get <u>the same</u> salary as her, but they have a <u>lot less</u> responsibility.

   _____

8. My life is <u>a lot</u> more interesting <u>than</u> it used to be.

   _____

9. As the day went on yesterday, I felt <u>more and more</u> worried.

   _____

10. My sister is nicer <u>than</u> my brother, but she doesn't have <u>as many</u> friends as him.

   _____

Although / though / even though   In spite of / despite

Complete the sentences, keeping the same meaning.

1. It was a cold day, but we went on a hike and enjoyed it.

   Even though _it was a cold day, we went on a hike and enjoyed it_____ .

2. It was a cold day, but we went on a hike and enjoyed it.

   In spite of _the cold (weather), we went on a hike and enjoyed it_____ .

3. It was a cold day, but we went on a hike and enjoyed it.

   _It was a cold day. We went on a hike and enjoyed it_____ , though.

4. She felt really sick, but my sister had to take care of my nephew.

   In spite of feeling _____ , _____ .

5. I didn't care for the lunch my aunt made, but I ate it anyway.

   Even though _____ .

6. I wasn't very busy yesterday, but I forgot to go to the bank.

   _____ . _____ , though.

7. My sister had a flu* shot, but she still got the flu.

   Even though _____ .

8. Rick answered her angrily, but Angela didn't show any anger herself.

   Despite Rick's angry _____ .

9. The United States spends more on health care than Canada, but it doesn't have a better health care system.

   Although _____ .

10. I wasn't very hungry, but I went to a restaurant with my friends.

    _____ . _____ , though.

11. Ana is having problems with her teenagers, but she manages to stay in a good mood*.

    Despite _____ , Ana _____ .

   * the flu (informal for *influenza*): *an infectious illness like a bad cold, bringing fever, pain, and weakness*
   * be in a good mood: *to be happy, friendly, content*

In case
Unless   As long as and *provided/providing*

Complete the sentences, keeping the same meaning.

1. I won't be able to finish this job if no one helps me with it.

   <u>*I won't be able to finish this job*</u>   unless <u>*someone helps me with it*</u>   .

2. As long as Pam isn't rude* to customers, she won't lose her job.

   Pam won't _____ unless _____ .

3. You should take extra money along on your trip. You might need it in San Francisco.

   _____ in case _____ .

4. The Suarez teenagers can stay out late, but they have to call home to say where they are.

   _____ as long as _____ .

5. I won't go running if it's raining in the morning.

   I _____ unless _____ .

6. Ted always leaves his phone number with the baby-sitter. She might need to contact him.

   _____ in case _____ .

7. You will get along with Angela, but be careful what you say to her.

   You _____ as long as _____ .

8. I can't go to the movies with you unless you pay my way*.

   _____ providing _____ .

9. Why don't you take your allergy* medicine along? You might need it.

   Why _____ in case _____ ?

10. My computer printer usually works well unless I've been using it too much.

    _____ if _____ .

11. I'll go to Hawaii with you if I have enough money.

    Provided _____ , I'll _____ .

* rude: *not polite; behaving in a way that hurts other people's feelings*
* pay someone's way: *to buy someone's ticket*
* allergy: *an illness that results from eating certain foods or contacting certain substances*

EXERCISE 138

UNITS
112-
114

As **(Time and Reason)**
Like **and** *as*
As if, as though, **and** *like*

Circle the correct word(s).

1. George works (as) / like a massage therapist.

2. <u>As</u> / <u>As if</u> you probably already know, Tim's getting married next month.

3. What's wrong? You look <u>as</u> / <u>as if</u> you had just seen a ghost.

4. The movie we saw last night didn't end <u>as</u> / <u>as though</u> I expected it to.

5. Chris works <u>as</u> / <u>like</u> a horse. That's why he's always tired at night.

6. Brendan felt foolish <u>just as</u> / <u>when</u> he realized his mistake.

7. <u>As</u> / <u>As if</u> I was brushing my teeth, a filling* came out of my tooth.

8. Sandy looks <u>as</u> / <u>like</u> she's had a hard day at work.

9. <u>Since</u> / <u>As though</u> you don't understand this, I'll explain it to you again.

10. You have a sense of humor <u>just as</u> / <u>like</u> my Uncle Bill's.

11. I don't know why the employees didn't do <u>as</u> / <u>as if</u> they were told.

12. The baby's acting <u>as</u> / <u>as though</u> she's sick.

13. I'm an adult. Please don't treat me <u>as</u> / <u>as if</u> I were a child.

14. If you ask me, you should wear livelier colors <u>as</u> / <u>like</u> blue and red.

15. Just <u>as</u> / <u>like</u> Amy got to work, her boss called her into his office.

16. That new singer sounds a lot <u>as</u> / <u>like</u> a singer from a long time ago.

17. Kathy speaks German <u>as</u> / <u>as if</u> she had grown up in Germany.

18. Stop it! You're acting <u>as</u> / <u>like</u> a child.

19. It smells <u>as</u> / <u>as if</u> someone is cooking fish.

20. Emily spoke <u>as</u> / <u>as if</u> she were angry with me.

21. The air got cooler and cooler <u>as</u> / <u>just as</u> we drove up the mountain.

22. Gina came to see us last night. She was full of news, <u>as</u> / <u>like</u> usual.

** filling: *a substance (e.g., gold, silver) put in a hole in a tooth*

EXERCISE 139

Like and *as*

Read the sayings and then read the situations. Write the letter of the situation which best illustrates each saying.

Sayings

1. It was like taking candy from a baby.   *d*

2. It's like looking for a needle in a haystack. _____

3. As the twig* is bent*, the tree will grow.   _____

4. Like father, like son.   _____

5. Do as I say, not as I do.   _____

6. They are like two peas in a pod*.   _____

7. Like a duck takes to water.   _____

Situations

a. Somehow I wasn't surprised when I heard that Matthew was getting divorced again. They say his father's been married four times!

b. You can't imagine how much Lisa looks and acts like her sister.

c. Abby, who's fifteen, wants to smoke with her friends. Her parents are really upset. They've told her she shouldn't smoke even though they smoke themselves.

✔d. It was easy to sneak* a note to my friend during class. I just waited until the teacher turned his back to write on the board.

e. Little Tyler will grow up to be a nice young man, I'm sure, because his parents are raising him very carefully.

f. "Did you have any trouble getting used to the food in Guatemala?" "Not at all. I loved it from the first bite."

g. We'll never find your ring on the beach. It's too small, and the beach is too big.

* twig: *a small thin branch of a tree*
* bent (past of *bend*): *shaped, formed*
* pod: *a long seed container that grows on some plants*
* sneak: *to do something secretly*

For, during, and *while*
By and *until*   *By the time . . .*

Circle the correct words to complete the paragraph.

I have a demanding* job and a wife and three children, so my days are very full and busy. I go to the health club after work three times **1)** (during)/ while the week to relax and relieve* stress. **2)** I exercise <u>during / for</u> about an hour at the club before going home. **3)** <u>During / While</u> I'm at the club, I try to work out* on the machines **4)** <u>during / for</u> about twenty minutes and swim **5)** <u>during / for</u> an equal amount of time. Sometimes the machines are all taken, so I run **6)** <u>during / while</u> I'm waiting for a machine. I exercise **7)** <u>by the time / until</u> I feel tired, and then I stop so that I don't overdo* it. Because I've been especially busy at work, I haven't gone to the club **8)** <u>during / for</u> three days, and I miss the exercise a lot. I need the exercise, but my family is very important to me, too.

Since my children don't go to sleep **9)** <u>by / until</u> 9 P.M., I still have time to see them when I get home. As long as I get home **10)** <u>by / until</u> 7:30, I can still eat dinner with my family and have time to talk to everyone before bedtime. **11)** <u>During / While</u> dinner, we discuss the events of the day and family matters. My wife and I don't go to bed **12)** <u>by / until</u> 11:30, so we have time together without the children, too. **13)** I have to get up <u>by / until</u> 6 A.M., so my day starts early. **14)** <u>By the time / Until</u> bedtime comes, I'm usually very tired and fall asleep fast.

* demanding: *that requires a lot of time, effort, or attention*
* relieve: *to make less bad*
* work out: *to exercise, especially with weights or on exercise machines*
* overdo: *to do something (exercise, work, etc.) too hard or for too long*

Use your own ideas to write new sentences with the words in parentheses.

1. (even though: car / old) Even though my car is old, it runs well.

   Even though he's not old enough to drive, my neighbors bought their son a car.

2. (in spite of: work / hard) In spite of my hard work, I didn't pass my exam.

3. (in case: need) My parents gave me some money in case I needed it on my trip.

4. (unless: do / angry) Some parents get angry unless their children do what the parents want.

5. (as long as: happy / job) I am happy as long as I have an interesting job and nice coworkers.

6. (provided: money / go) I will probably go to England next summer provided I have enough money.

7. (as: get / older) As my parents get older, they travel more than before.

8. (like: most people) Like most people, I have to work to live.

9. (as though: sometimes / feel) Sometimes I feel as though I can't finish all the work I have to do.

10. (as if: were / new) I bought a used car, but it looks and runs as if it were new.

At/on/in (Time)
On time / in time, at the end / in the end

Prepositions

Write *at*, *on*, or *in*. Use *X* if no word is needed.

1. a. Many Americans get married __in__ June.

   b. My brother got married _____ June 4, 1993.

   c. Not many people get married _____ the morning, but it's possible.

2. a. I don't like to travel _____ the winter.

   b. I took a wonderful trip with friends _____ last August.

3. a. Experts say it's better not to exercise _____ the end of the day.

   b. Do you have more energy _____ the morning or _____ night?

   c. Would you like to play tennis _____ this Saturday?

4. a. A lot of diseases have been eradicated* _____ the last 100 years.

   b. Many diseases that were a problem _____ the past are no longer a problem.

   c. A lot of medical research is being done on AIDS and cancer _____ this time.

   d. _____ the nineteenth century and before, people died of diseases that are seldom fatal* today.

   e. Of course, serious new diseases like AIDS may emerge _____ the future.

5. a. Scott isn't very punctual*. He seldom gets to work _____ time.

   b. Did you get to work _____ time for your meeting?

   c. We got stuck* in traffic, so we didn't make it to the wedding _____ time. We were a little late.

6. a. _____ first I didn't understand Julia's question, but she made it clear _____ the end.

   b. At my office, we usually have more work _____ the end of the year than _____ the beginning.

   c. The boss gives us a bonus* _____ every December.

* eradicate: *to put an end to*
* fatal: *causing death*
* punctual: *seldom being late*
* stuck (past participle of *stick*): *not able to move*
* bonus: *extra money given as a present or reward*

EXERCISE 143

In/at/on (Place)

Complete the sentences. Use *in*, *at*, or *on*.

1. Mary didn't come to work __*on*__ her bike today. I saw her __*in*__ a car.

2. Poor Claudia is sick _____ bed _____ home again.

3. Would you rather spend your free time _____ a concert or _____ a movie?

4. I was _____ a meeting from 8 till 11 yesterday morning.

5. I don't think I'll have time to eat lunch _____ my usual restaurant before my trip, so I'll just eat something _____ the plane tonight.

6. Did you stay _____ your cousin's place _____ the mountains or her place _____ the coast?

7. I have a friend who would rather be _____ work than _____ home. Imagine!

8. My father met your boss _____ a party _____ a ship.

9. Is it safer for a child to sit _____ the back of the car or _____ the front?

10. Don't you want to write your return address _____ the back of the envelope before I mail the letter?

11. I had to stand _____ line for twenty minutes _____ the post office to buy stamps.

12. It's starting to rain. Let's wait _____ the post office until it stops.

13. Chicago isn't _____ the Mississippi River; it's _____ Lake Michigan.

14. Did you see that strange name "Kalamazoo" _____ a map or _____ a book?

15. Jason lives _____ a busy street _____ the first floor, so his place is noisy.

16. George doesn't have time to work now that he's _____ law school.

17. I never got used to driving _____ the left when I was in Tokyo.

18. Glen couldn't find his watch because he had put it _____ a small table _____ the corner. He didn't see it there.

UNITS
122-
124

To/at/in/into
On/in/at (Other Uses)
By

Complete the sentences. Use the words in parentheses and *in*, *by*, *on*, or *with*.

1. (taxi / foot) I went <u>*by taxi*</u> because I was too tired to go
   <u>*on foot*</u> .

2. (my car) Let's go downtown _____ . (bus) It takes too long
   _____ .

3. (someone / a stone) The window was broken _____
   _____ .

4. (check / cash) I like to pay bills _____ rather than
   _____ so that I have a record of the payment.

5. (a very good camera / a professional) This picture was obviously taken
   _____ _____ .

6. (TV / countless people) The World Cup is watched _____
   _____ .

7. Don't be angry with Ted. (accident) He took your book _____ .
   (purpose) He didn't do it _____ .

8. (my car) I waited for an hour _____ . (the five o'clock train) My father
   was supposed to be _____ , but he didn't come until after 6.

9. (hand / my aunt) This sweater was made _____ .

10. (the American writer Arthur Miller / the radio) They are presenting a play
    _____ this week.

EXERCISE 145

To/at/in/into
On/in/at (Other Uses)
By

Complete the conversations. Use the words in parentheses and *at*, *by*, *in*, *into*, *on*, *to*, or *with*. Use an appropriate tense.

1. *A:* Why is the boss mad at you?

   B: (get / work late this morning) Because I ___got to work late this morning___ .

2. *A:* *(husband to wife in a hotel)* Why isn't our room ready?

   B: (arrive / the hotel early) Because we _____ .

3. *A:* Shall we take my car?

   B: No. (go / my car) Let's _____ . It's bigger.

4. *A:* Did you see Mark and Jan when you were in Seattle?

   B: (be away / vacation last week) No, they _____

   _____ .

5. *A:* Do you drive to work?

   B: (be / cheaper and faster / subway) No, it _____

   _____ .

6. *A:* How did you go shopping if your car was at the mechanic's? Did you walk?

   B: (go / my bike) No, _____ .

7. *A:* Why don't we go somewhere we've never been before on vacation?

   B: Good idea. How about Miami? (never be / Florida) We _____

   _____ .

8. *A:* Why doesn't Helen drive to work? Isn't it far?

   B: (can't get / her small car) Because with her back injury, she _____

   _____ very easily.

9. *A:* You look tired this morning. Didn't you sleep well?

   B: (go / bed late last night) Not long enough. I _____ .

10. *A:* How did you fix that broken dish?

    B: (fix it / glue) I _____ .

Use the words in parentheses to complete the conversations. Add the correct prepositions. Use the simple present tense.

1. *A:* Why was the train late?

   B: (not / know the reason / the delay) I <u>don't know the reason for the delay</u> .

2. *A:* Do you think soccer is becoming more popular in the U.S.?

   B: (there / be / an increase / the number of fans) Yes, <u>there is an increase in the</u>
   <u>number of fans</u> every year.

3. *A:* Will it take long to repair the damage from the storm?

   B: (the damage / many buildings / be / extensive) Yes, _____
   _____ .

4. *A:* Why are Jim and Dave arguing?

   B: (the cause / the argument / not be / clear to me) _____
   _____ .

5. *A:* What do the flood* victims* need?

   B: (there / be / an urgent need / blankets and clothes) _____
   _____ .

6. *A:* The city has been discussing the water problem for years, hasn't it?

   B: (it / not / be / easy to find a solution / the problem) Yes, because _____
   _____ .

7. *Teacher:* Don't you want to answer Question 17? You left it blank.

   Student: (not / know / the answer / that question) No, I _____
   _____ .

8. *A:* Why doesn't Roger see his father more often? They live in the same town.

   B: (his relationship / his father / not / be / very good) _____
   _____ .

* flood: *large amount of water covering a large area of land that is usually dry*
* victim: *a person hurt or killed in a disaster, a crime, etc.*

ITS
26-
27

Adjective + Preposition

Complete the sentences. Use an adjective in the box and the correct preposition.

ashamed	capable	different	generous	~~impressed~~
jealous	responsible	satisfied	silly	worried

1. The museum was *impressed with* the artist's work, so it bought a painting.

2. You told your father a lie? You should be _____ yourself!

3. An only child can be very _____ a new baby in the family.

4. Are you _____ my work, or do you want me to do it again?

5. Who is _____ children's character – their parents or their teachers?

6. I can't thank you enough. You have been very _____ me.

7. It was _____ me not to lock my car, but I was only gone for
   five minutes.

8. Hannah's a good athlete, but I don't think she's _____ running the
   800 meters in two minutes.

9. What's wrong? You look _____ something.

10. You won't recognize Stanley now. He looks a lot _____ before.

UNITS
126-127

Adjective + Preposition

Complete the sentences, keeping the same meaning. Use the preposition that goes with the adjective given. Be sure to use an appropriate form of *be*.

1. Jessica still gets money from her father.

   Jessica ___*is*___ still dependent ___*on her father for money*___ .

2. Do you want to go on a hike?

   ___*Are*___ you interested ___*in going on a hike*___ ?

3. I don't trust people who talk too much.

   I _____ suspicious _____ .

4. The store didn't have much milk.

   The store _____ short _____ .

5. My problem is almost the same as yours.

   _____ similar _____ .

6. Dogs frighten Joy a lot.

   _____ very afraid _____ .

7. I'm sorry I yelled at you yesterday.

   _____ sorry _____ .

8. My Brazilian friend likes fruit a lot.

   _____ very fond _____ .

9. Linda has no interest in school.

   _____ bored _____ .

10. Our teacher doesn't have much tolerance for students who come to class late.

    _____ not very tolerant _____ .

11. Paul isn't a very good baseball player.

    Paul _____ very good _____ .

EXERCISE 149

Verb + Preposition – *at* and *to*
Verb + Preposition – *about/for/of/after*

Complete the sentences. Use one of the verbs in the box in the correct form + *at*, *to*, *about*, *for*, or *of*.

apologize	apply	ask	care	care	explain	explain
invite	look	~~look~~	shout	take care	talk	throw

1. Why are you *looking at* _____ me like that? I didn't do anything.

2. Claudia _____ "hello" _____ me from the back of the bus yesterday.

3. (*on the phone*) May I _____ Mr. Smith, please?

4. *A:* Who's _____ your baby while you're shopping?
   B: My mother is.

5. I _____ ice at the supermarket, but I couldn't find it anywhere.

6. Brandon couldn't _____ me how to start up* my computer.

7. In some places people _____ rice _____ the bride and groom after the wedding ceremony.

8. Freddie _____ his aunt for forgetting her invitation to dinner last week.

9. *A:* Would you _____ a little more to eat?
   B: No, thanks. I'm full.

10. Teenagers often _____ a lot _____ how they look. Clothes are important to them.

11. Do you want me to _____ your boss _____ the party?

12. Can you _____ the meaning of this word _____ me?

13. Jessica is always _____ me _____ money, but I never give her any.

14. Nicholas has _____ several colleges, and two have accepted him.

* start up: *turn on*

Verb + Preposition – *at* and *to*
Verb + Preposition – *about/for/of/after*

Complete the sentences. Use the words in parentheses in the correct order. Put in the correct preposition(s) where needed.

1. (what happened / me) Could you explain _to me what happened_ again?

2. (this bread / the birds) Would you please throw _this bread to the birds_ ?

3. (me / your house) Could you describe _____ ?

4. (it) Stop worrying about the storm. There's nothing we can do _____ .

5. (them) Let's not buy carrots. I don't care _____ .

6. (your problem) I think we need to have a long discussion _____ .

7. (the airport) Your flight's at six? What time do you have to leave _____ ?

8. (when we eat) We can eat now or later. I don't care _____ .

9. (how he felt / the doctor) It was difficult for Pete to describe _____
   _____ .

10. (what I'm saying) Please pay attention. You're not listening _____ .

11. (a used car) It's a good idea to take a good look _____ before
    buying it.

12. (your appearance) When you're sick, it's hard to care _____ .

13. (Jason) I can't go out yet. I'm waiting _____ to return
    my call.

14. (why he didn't vote / us) Stan doesn't want to explain _____
    _____ .

15. (the teacher / her problem) Sylvia's English wasn't good enough to explain _____
    _____ .

16. (himself) Poor old Mr. Brown needs to look _____ better. He
    doesn't eat very well.

Verb + Preposition – *about* and *of*
Verb + Preposition – *of/for/from/on*

Complete the sentences, keeping the same meanings. Include *about*, *of*, *for*, *from*, or *on*. Make any necessary changes.

1. My dream is to go to Egypt someday

   I dream *of going to Egypt* _____ someday.

2. That man looks like someone I know.

   That man reminds _____ .

3. Amy complained that her new car cost too much.

   _____ that she'd paid too much _____ .

4. Hannah hasn't written or called me since last summer.

   I haven't heard _____ .

5. More Americans have heart disease than cancer.

   _____ suffer _____ .

6. My brother might move to San Francisco.

   My brother is thinking _____ .

7. My roommate said that I was lazy.

   My roommate accused _____ .

8. That child eats almost nothing besides cereal and milk.

   _____ practically lives _____ .

9. This sunscreen will keep you from getting a sunburn.

   _____ will protect your skin _____ the sun.

10. The radio usually tells people when there are serious weather conditions.

    The radio usually warns _____ .

11. The name of that restaurant escapes me.

    I can't think _____ .

12. Don't say that your problems are my fault.

    Don't blame _____ problems.

Match the two halves of the sentences. Write the letter of the second half next to the first half.

_d_ 1. Your confidence will increase if you believe

_____ 2. With all this noise, it's hard for me to concentrate

_____ 3. Fortunately, no one was hurt when the two cars collided

_____ 4. When he was learning to drive, Chris drove

_____ 5. For moderate* exercise, many people prefer swimming

_____ 6. My company supplies employees

_____ 7. I doubt Angela will ever succeed

_____ 8. For this recipe, you need to cut everything

_____ 9. I offered to help, but Sandy insisted

_____ 10. My language skills aren't good enough to translate this letter

_____ 11. I knew I had hurt my brother when his eyes filled

_____ 12. The Careys have no idea when their house was broken

_____ 13. Bad things sometimes happen

_____ 14. I don't like to spend money

_____ 15. Mr. Grimes doesn't believe

_____ 16. To be fair, Mother divided the chocolate

a. into the mailbox.

b. in getting her husband to stop snoring.

c. into Arabic.

✔d. in yourself.

e. on silly things.

f. to good people.

g. with uniforms but not with shoes.

h. into equal parts.

i. in spending a lot of money on clothes.

j. with each other.

k. into small pieces.

l. into.

m. on changing the tire alone.

n. to more vigorous* activities.

o. on this letter I'm writing.

p. with tears.

* moderate: *neither too much nor too little*
* vigorous: *strong, active*

Phrasal Verbs (*get up / break down / fill in*, etc.)

Complete the conversations. Use one of the verbs in the box in the correct form and a pronoun.

break down	fill out	~~give back~~	look up	put out
see off	show around	throw away	try on	wake up

1. *A:* If I lend you my tools, when will I get them back?

   B: I'll _give them back_____ to you by next Friday at the latest.

2. *A:* Did you buy the jeans that were on sale?

   B: No. I _____, but they didn't fit.

3. *A:* Bob took you to the airport? Didn't he have to work?

   B: He was supposed to, but he wanted to _____ .

4. *A:* Are you whispering* because the children are asleep?

   B: Yes, I don't want to _____ .

5. *A:* I'm surprised you didn't enjoy San Francisco.

   B: Well, our friends weren't there to _____
   the city, and we didn't know what to visit.

6. *A:* Are you still confused about *lie* and *lay*?

   B: No, I _____ in a dictionary yesterday.

7. *A:* Can't I smoke this cigarette here?

   B: No, I'm afraid you'll have to _____ .

8. *A:* Have you seen yesterday's newspaper?

   B: Sorry. I _____ .

9. *A:* How did the firefighters get in the burning building if the door was locked?

   B: They had to _____ .

10. *A:* Have you finished all your job applications?

    B: Yes, I finished _____ last night.

   *whisper: *to speak in a soft voice*

Phrasal Verbs (*get up / break down / fill in*, etc.)

Complete the sentences. Use one of the verbs in the box in the correct form + *away,*
by, down, off, on, out, **or** *up.*

calm	cross	doze	drop	fill	get	give
keep	make	show	throw	~~turn~~	turn	

1. When you go out, please *turn* _____ the lights _*off*_____ .

2. I can't go to the movies. I have two application forms that I need to _____
   _____ tonight.

3. The cup is broken. I'm going to _____ it _____ .

4. I don't have that book of poetry anymore. I _____ it _____
   months ago. A friend wanted it.

5. Eric lost his job. I hope he and his wife can _____ _____ on
   just one salary.

6. All the workers were supposed to go to the meeting, but only a few _____
   _____ .

7. Is that a true story, or are you _____ it _____ ?

8. Adam will never find a good job if he _____ _____ of high
   school at sixteen.

9. I'm sure the army will _____ Sean _____ because of his heart
   problems. They want soldiers in good health.

10. My grandfather frequently _____ _____ while he's watching
    TV, especially after dinner.

11. Try to _____ _____ . I know you're upset, but shouting
    won't help.

12. Your name was on the list yesterday, but someone has _____ it
    _____ .

13. Computers change so fast that I can't _____ _____ with all
    the improvements.

REVIEW
Prepositions

Use your own ideas to write sentences with both of the prepositional phrases in parentheses.

1. (in the last century / in the future)

   There will be more pollution in the future than there was in the last century.
   _____

2. (at the same time / on weekends) _____

   On weekends, to relax I sometimes read and listen to music at the same time.
   _____

3. (in the end / on time) _____

   I didn't think I was going to be on time, but in the end I got there early.
   _____

4. (in the house / in the yard) _____
   _____

5. (in my opinion / to prison) _____
   _____

6. (in the hospital / on a bicycle) _____
   _____

7. (on the way to . . . / by accident) _____
   _____

8. (in the world / on the right) _____
   _____

9. (on the ground / at a table) _____
   _____

10. (on the whole / on purpose) _____
    _____

EXERCISE 156

UNITS
*125-
132*

REVIEW
Prepositions

Use your own ideas to complete the sentences.

1. I spend most of my money on *clothes* OR *rent and food* OR *going out*   .
   I spend most of my money on _____.

2. I don't believe in *lending people money* OR *ghosts*   .
   I don't believe in _____.

3. I made a mistake. It was silly of me to _____
   _____

4. I can always rely on _____ when
   _____.

5. There are many things I'd like to do in my life. I sometimes dream of _____
   _____.

6. I am different from _____ because
   I _____.

7. I don't normally care for _____.

8. It would make me very happy to get news from _____.

9. I wish the government would do something about _____.

10. I sometimes get upset about some people's attitude toward _____
    _____.

11. I am fond of _____ , but I'm not very good at it.

12. I enjoy talking to _____ more than to anyone else because
    _____.

13. Sometimes people compliment me on _____.

Answer Key

In some of the exercises, you have to use your own ideas to write answers. If possible, check your answers with someone who speaks English well.

EXERCISE 1

A

2. 's not / isn't getting (is not getting) better
3. 'm making (am making) a salad
4. are painting the bedrooms
5. 's taking (is taking) a shower
6. 'm having (am having) a good time
7. 's studying (is studying) law
8. 's improving (is improving) all the time

B

2. The doctor is; 's not / isn't (is not) getting better
3. 'm cutting (am cutting) tomatoes because I'm making (I am making) a salad
4. The Lee children are spending the night at a friend's house because their parents are painting the bedrooms

EXERCISE 2

2. swims in a pool every morning
3. studies in the library
4. Her older sister takes care of her.
5. She works in a bank.
6. don't drink (do not drink) coffee
7. She doesn't like (does not like) him.
8. He usually drives his car.
9. looks angry today
10. I exercise once or twice a week.

EXERCISE 3

2. feel dizzy
3. it rains
4. Yes, I change jobs
5. Yes, he/she travels abroad
6. Yes, they move
7. Yes, she washes her windows
8. Yes, I have trouble with my car
9. Yes, he cooks fish for dinner
10. Yes, they watch soap operas on TV

EXERCISE 4

1. 'm not working (am not working)
2. Is he doing; 's talking (is talking)
3. 're going out (are going out)
4. you take; usually get; isn't driving (is not driving)
5. are visiting
6. doesn't flow (does not flow)
7. are you shouting
8. 's getting (is getting); Do you want
9. Do you usually leave; 'm leaving (am leaving)
10. 's always complaining (is always complaining); don't want (do not want)
11. Does it belong

EXERCISE 5

2. 'm making (am making); need
3. Do; see
4. is; think
5. Are; having; love
6. tastes; looks
7. 's (is); prefer
8. 's thinking (is thinking); wants
9. does; mean; have
10. belongs; contains
11. don't realize (do not realize); 're being (are being)
12. Are; using

EXERCISE 6

4. I forgot his name.
5. Did you see the sunset last night?
6. The baby didn't eat (did not eat) all her breakfast.
7. Were you on time for work yesterday?
8. They didn't sell (did not sell) their house for a good price.
9. You spent too much money on your haircut.
10. Amy lost her ring, but she found it.
11. How did Ann catch a cold?
12. Martin didn't teach (did not teach) last night because it was a holiday.
13. The book cost a lot, but I bought it anyway.
14. Did anyone get hurt in the accident?

EXERCISE 7

2. wasn't walking (was not walking)
3. weren't working (were not working) for a computer company the last time I saw
4. weren't taking (were not taking) a Chinese cooking class the last time I saw them
5. He wasn't exercising (was not exercising) five days a week the last time I saw him.
6. You weren't thinking (were not thinking) of moving to Toronto the last time I saw you.
7. She wasn't making (was not making) commercials the last time I saw her.
8. He wasn't having (was not having) trouble at work the last time I saw him.
9. You weren't talking (were not talking) about adopting a baby the last time I saw you.
10. You weren't working (were not working) at home two days a week the last time I saw you.

11. They weren't having (were not having) problems with their children the last time I saw them.

3. happened
4. didn't see (did not see)
5. slowed
6. stopped
7. didn't notice (did not notice)
8. was talking
9. was sitting
10. turned
11. drove
12. was crossing
13. tried
14. was
15. hit
16. was
17. were moving
18. got out
19. checked
20. spoke
21. had
22. arrived
23. made
24. happened
25. thought

EXERCISE 9

3. went
4. attended
5. got
6. was
7. asked
8. have
9. are
10. live
11. visit
12. are
13. spend
14. plan
15. grew
16. enjoyed
17. own
18. came
19. were working
20. 're doing (are doing)
21. know
22. don't have (do not have)
23. is growing
24. borrowed
25. want
26. 're paying (are paying)

EXERCISE 10

Answers will vary.

EXERCISE 11

2. a
3. c
4. c
5. a
6. b
7. c
8. a

EXERCISE 12

2. 's never happened (has never happened) to me
3. she's changed (she has changed)
4. Have you seen Dr. Abbott about your cold yet?
5. She's already left (She has already left).
6. hasn't gotten (has not gotten) it yet
7. Have you done anything interesting recently?
8. you've eaten (you have eaten) at this restaurant
9. hasn't been (has not been)

EXERCISE 13

3. 've been taking (have been taking) aspirin every day
4. 've been fixing (have been fixing) the streets in the area
5. 've been taking (have been taking) classes at the college
6. 've been traveling (have been traveling) a lot on business
7. 've been going (have been going) to a new one
8. 's been raining (has been raining) here
9. 've been waiting (have been waiting) to see her
10. 've been saving (have been saving) money

EXERCISE 14

2. 's written (has written) six letters so far
3. How long have you been doing your homework?; 've been studying (have been studying) since breakfast
4. How much money has she spent today?; She's spent (She has spent) a lot of money.
5. How long have they been dancing?; They've been dancing (They have been dancing) all evening.
6. How many times have you played cards this week?; 've played (have played) three times.
7. How many rooms has he painted today?; He's finished (He has finished) three rooms.

EXERCISE 15

A

3. I've been waiting (I have been waiting) for a long time.
4. She's been (She has been) a judge since last year.
5. He got married several months ago.
6. We've lived (We have lived) here for about three years
7. We lived in Cleveland for a year before that

8. It's been raining (It has been raining) since the day before yesterday.
9. bought a new TV since 1990

B

3. How long have you been sick?
4. How long have you lived near school?
5. When did you start your new job?
6. How long has your brother lived in Egypt?
7. When did he leave the office?

EXERCISE 16

Answers will vary.
Sample answers:
3. I took a vacation
4. Jeff and Susan have been living in Boston
5. I have worked for the same company
6. I have lived in the same town
7. My brother got his law degree
8. The Robinsons have owned their restaurant
9. I have made a lot of progress
10. I have known Lillian
11. Richard and I have been friends
12. My family moved from Europe to the United States
13. My father worked as an actor
14. I visited my relatives in South America
15. I haven't called my mother
16. I went to the gym three times
17. I have gone to the gym once

EXERCISE 17

3. She'd been (She had been) away for several years. We had a long talk.
4. I'd worked (I had worked) very hard at the office. I didn't brush (did not brush) my teeth before going to bed.
5. Everyone was happy for them. They'd known (They had known) each other for a long time.
6. It was difficult for him.
   He'd never done (He had never done) it before.
7. Linda had gone to bed early. The doorbell woke her.

EXERCISE 18

A

3. he'd been studying (he had been studying) all night
4. she'd been drinking (she had been drinking) coffee all morning
5. she'd been jogging (she had been jogging) in the afternoon
6. she was studying for a test
7. he was planting flowers in the garden
8. he'd been cooking (he had been cooking)

B

2. Sarah didn't see (did not see) the accident because she was looking at her watch.

3. Roger's eyes were so red this morning because he'd been studying (he had been studying) all night.
4. Kate didn't want (did not want) any tea this afternoon because she'd been drinking (she had been drinking) coffee all morning.
5. Jennifer was so tired at dinner last night because she'd been jogging (she had been jogging) in the afternoon.

EXERCISE 19

4. have a stomachache or 've got (have got) a stomachache
5. Have a safe trip
6. don't have (do not have) enough money or haven't got enough money
7. had trouble
8. doesn't have (does not have) many friends or hasn't got many friends
9. Did; have fun
10. have some water to drink
11. Did he have an operation

EXERCISE 20

3. Mark used to be good looking [when he was younger].
4. I used to smoke [ten years ago].
5. Mr. Simpson used to be a good father. or Mr. Simpson didn't use to be [did not use to be] a bad father
6. I used to eat a lot of candy.
7. My sister used to work at that hospital.
8. Glen and I used to be good friends.
9. I used to sleep late. or I didn't use to get (did not use to get) up early.
10. Al and Anne used to be a happy couple.
11. Mrs. Finley didn't use to have (did not use to have) trouble walking.
12. We used to have a beautiful Persian carpet.
13. My neighbors used to go out to eat all the time. or My neighbors didn't use to eat (did not use to eat) at home much.

EXERCISE 21

Answers will vary.
Sample answers:
1. I have been saving for a car for a long time.
2. I have traveled to Italy, but I have never been to Rome.
3. My grandparents have been married for 50 years.
4. We just moved to this town, and we don't know many people here yet.
5. My sister is very excited. She has been that way since she found a new job.
6. I've already shopped for groceries today, so I don't need to go to the store again.
7. I haven't been to the new museum.

8. My brother has been learning how to cook, but he hasn't learned how to make bread.
9. I haven't seen my uncle and aunt since I was little.
10. My friends and I haven't been playing soccer in the park recently.
11. It's been a long time since I ate meat.

EXERCISE 22

2. hadn't eaten
3. was feeding
4. wanted
5. stopped
6. realized
7. were watching
8. had spent
9. was
10. was
11. didn't brag
12. got
13. had
14. felt
15. had eaten
16. arranged
17. have decided

EXERCISE 23

2. B: it arrives at 1:25; Are you meeting someone on the flight?
3. A: When are you getting married?
   B: And we're spending (we are spending) our honeymoon in Hawaii.
4. A: Are you riding home with me?
   B: The last one runs at midnight.
5. A: Are you doing anything tonight?
   B: I'm doing (I am doing) my grocery shopping.
   A: Daniel and I are going to the movies.
6. A: Are you picking me up from school today?
7. A: I'm taking (I am taking) a 7 o'clock flight

EXERCISE 24

A

3. 're going to take (are going to take) a long trip in it
4. 's going to have (is going to have) an accident
5. 's going to be (is going to be) sorry
6. I'm going to quit (I am going to quit) soon.
7. They're going to have (They are going to have) a party. *or* Adrienne and Todd are going to have . . .
8. When are we going to fix them?

B

2. My brother was going to visit me
3. You were going to help me last night
4. My parents were going to take a trip
5. I was going to sell my car

EXERCISE 25

2. is going to quit
3. doesn't open
4. am visiting *or* am going to visit
5. are getting out *or* are going to get out
6. is going to rain
7. is going to burn
8. am taking care of *or* am going to take care of
9. is coming *or* is going to come
10. Are you having *or* Are you going to have
11. am not giving *or* am not going to give
12. isn't going to teach

EXERCISE 26

2. 'll return (will return) them next week
3. Will you please shut the door?
4. My computer won't start (will not start).
5. I'll spend (I will spend) my extra money on one
6. 'll explain (will explain) the word to you
7. 'll need (will need) warm clothes
8. I won't do (will not) do it again.

EXERCISE 27

2. 'll be (will be) a good race
3. will finish the race
4. will do well in the race
5. who will win the race
6. he'll probably get (he will probably get) a good place to stand

EXERCISE 28

3. are going to move
4. 'll come (will come)
5. He's going to lose (he is going to lose)
6. 'm going to stop (am going to stop)
7. 'll buy (will buy)
8. are going to have
9. 'll make (will make)
10. 'm going to go (am going to go)
11. They aren't (are not) / They're not (They are not) going to get

EXERCISE 29

2. a; b
3. a; c; d
4. b; d
5. a; b; d
6. a; c

EXERCISE 30

4. stops
5. go
6. will call
7. finds out
8. don't get (do not get)

9. reaches
10. won't paint (will not paint)
11. moves
12. decide
13. 'll regret (will regret)
14. 'll feel (will feel)
15. won't bother (will not bother)

EXERCISE 31

Answers will vary.

EXERCISE 32

3. can't go (cannot go) out for a week
4. I couldn't find (I could not find) my wallet
5. can't see (cannot see) the screen very well
6. could hear airplanes all night
7. can play several musical instruments
8. Can you speak
9. couldn't do (could not do) anything to help

EXERCISE 33

3. were able to
4. couldn't (could not) *or* wasn't able to (was not able to)
5. could *or* was able to
6. was able to
7. was able to
8. couldn't (could not) *or* wasn't able to (was not able to)
9. couldn't (could not) *or* weren't able to (were not able to)
10. were able to

EXERCISE 34

2. was able to find; couldn't find
3. couldn't speak; can have
4. could hear
5. can't go
6. could mean
7. hasn't been able to find
8. was able to get
9. could have stayed
10. was finally able to get
11. can be
12. couldn't taste
13. couldn't understand

EXERCISE 35

4. must go to church [on Sunday mornings]
5. They must not be here [this week]. *or* Jack and Alice must not be here [this week].
6. must not be running well these days
7. She must have gotten divorced. *or* Sheila must have gotten divorced.
8. must be bothering him

9. must not have been at work last Friday
10. He must have been thinking about something else. *or* Al must have been thinking . . .

EXERCISE 36

2. may drive
3. may have gone
4. might be taking
5. might have gone
6. couldn't have been
7. might have left
8. may have had
9. couldn't have taken
10. might be having

EXERCISE 37

A

4. The post office may/might not deliver mail on the Presidents' Day holiday.
5. Your son may/might be trying to call you right now.
6. Tom may/might have forgotten to call his grandparents.
7. The Hennigans may/might have sold their car to buy something else.
8. Carol may/might not have been kidding when she said she was sick.

B

2. I might have to work this weekend.
3. I might be able to help you Saturday if I don't have to work.
4. You might not have to give me a ride after all.

EXERCISE 38

2. 2. may/might have forgotten it at school
3. 1. may/might miss her boyfriend *or* may/might be missing her boyfriend
   2. She may/might have had an argument with her father. *or* Sarah . . .
4. 1. may/might be worried about something
   2. He may/might have eaten a lot for lunch. *or* Reggie . . .
5. 1. may/might be doing something else tonight
   2. She may/might have forgotten about the party. *or* Rose . . .
6. 1. may/might be at the mechanic's
   2. may/might have sold his car
7. 1. may/might not have seen the other car
   2. She may/might have been thinking of something else. *or* Angela . . .

EXERCISE 39

2. have got to
3. must
4. don't have to
5. must not

6. don't have to
7. must not
8. had to
9. have got to
10. had to
11. have got to
12. don't have to

EXERCISE 40

3. I had to work late last night
4. my wife has to go to a meeting
5. he had to go back to work
6. I didn't have to pay (did not have to pay) anything
7. I have to call my travel agent about my plane tickets
8. Did you have to go to the hospital last night?
9. We don't have to return (do not have to return) it.
10. Do you have to have a driver's license to drive in your country?

EXERCISE 41

4. should have bought
5. should get
6. should be working; shouldn't be taking (should not be takng)
7. should have been studying
8. should have been
9. shouldn't have (should not have)
10. shouldn't have been talking (should not have been talking)
11. should have returned
12. should think

EXERCISE 42

3. [that] he put a pillow under his leg to be more comfortable *or* [that] Jerry put . . .
4. [that] he drink a lot of milk to help his bones heal *or* [that] Jerry drink . . .
5. [that] he call him/her every day to get the homework *or* [that] Jerry call . . .
6. [that] he take aspirin if his leg hurts a lot *or* [that] Jerry take . . .
7. [that] he not walk on his leg for a few days *or* [that] Jerry not walk . . .

EXERCISE 43

2. 'd better see (had better see) a dentist soon.
3. 'd better not send (had better not send) the letter that way
4. 'd better get (had better get) more food
5. 'd better not break (had better not break) his promise
6. 'd better play (had better play) later
7. 'd better call (had better call) my aunt today
8. 'd better stop and buy (had better stop and buy) some gas

EXERCISE 44

A

3. had better
4. should
5. had better
6. had better
7. should
8. should

B

2. bought
3. It's time we did something about the homeless people in this country.
4. It's time we went
5. It's time you were more
6. It's time we had

EXERCISE 45

3. could
4. Would you like
5. Can/May I
6. Can/Could/Would you
7. Would you like
8. Can/May I
9. you could
10. I could
11. Can/Could/May I
12. you could
13. Would you like to

EXERCISE 46

Answers will vary.
Sample answers:
1. I could stay up until 10 o'clock
2. finish my assignment for English class
3. be out of town
4. always use your seat belt
5. my coworker; finished my report without her help
6. quit my job
7. babysit for my little sister
8. run three or four times a week
9. a leak in the ceiling of our apartment; find the leak and fix it
10. visit Brazil for its beaches
11. baked a cake
12. cleaned our refrigerator
13. forgotten our appointment
14. have accident insurance
15. eat fewer sweets

EXERCISE 47

Answers will vary.
Sample answers:
1. My friends must be out of town because they haven't answered my calls.

2. This city should have more programs and build more centers for senior citizens.
3. The mechanic must not be busy. He said he could fix my car today.
4. I'm good at math, so I don't have to spend a lot of time balancing my checkbook.
5. My brother was playing computer games. He should have been cleaning the garage.
6. The newspaper carrier might not have delivered the paper yet today. I don't see it on the stairs or in the yard.
7. My husband has to write a paper for his economics class, so we may not be able to come to your party this weekend.
8. The paint is coming off the windows. It's time we repainted our house.
9. My teacher didn't insist that I take the writing class this term, but she recommended that I take it next term

EXERCISE 48

3. he would be more efficient
4. people would work harder
5. if he answered questions clearly
6. we could go home on time
7. if he didn't get (did not get) angry for no reason
8. if he didn't change his mind [so much]
9. if he were a good boss

EXERCISE 49

3. he worked in an office
4. weren't raining (were not raining) outside right now
5. wish they could afford a new car
6. wishes he lived near the ocean
7. wishes she were married
8. wishes she didn't have (did not have) thirteen cats
9. wish they didn't have to get up (did not have to get up) so early

EXERCISE 50

3. If it hadn't been (had not been) a stormy day, they'd have gone (they would have gone) swimming.
4. If she hadn't been (had not been) outside the classroom, she'd have heard (she would have heard) the teacher's announcement.
5. If he'd been feeling (he had been feeling) well, he'd have eaten (he would have eaten) breakfast.
6. If they'd been (they had been) at home, they would have received the package.
7. If she hadn't been (she had not been) on her bike, she'd have stopped (she would have stopped) to buy groceries.
8. If he'd been able to find (he had been able to find) his dictionary, he'd have been able to look up (he would have been able to look up) the new word in the dictionary.

EXERCISE 51

3. had accepted it
4. had been more considerate
5. had told me
6. had thought of it
7. I wish I hadn't spent (had not spent) so much money on my car.
8. I wish I had brought my umbrella this morning.
9. I wish I hadn't listened (had not listened) to his advice.
10. he had had more time to think about it
11. I wish I had been able to go.

EXERCISE 52

2. make his bed
3. wouldn't leave (would not leave) his clothes on the floor
4. wouldn't stay up (would not stay up) late
5. get angry [with me] about the messy room
6. wouldn't be (would not be) so bossy
7. wouldn't tell (would not tell) me to make my bed
8. I wish he wouldn't blame (would not blame) me for the mess in our room. *or* I wish Ted wouldn't blame (would not blame) . . .
9. I wish he wouldn't act (would not act) like a father. *or* I wish Ted would not act . . .
10. I wish he wouldn't go (would not go) to bed so early. *or* I wish Ted would not go . . .

EXERCISE 53

Answers will vary.
Sample answers:
1. had a job; get my own apartment
2. was a big supermarket near my house
3. My wife wishes I would get a better-paying job.
4. I could go out with my friends more often if I didn't have class three nights a week.
5. I wouldn't have gone to the film if I had known about the bad reviews.
6. I wish I had studied more for the English exam.
7. If I had realized that Martha was in town, I would have called her last night.
8. My mother would always tell me that you had to be a friend in order to have friends.
9. I wish I hadn't spent so much money on clothes and CDs.

EXERCISE 54

2. Mrs. Chen's dog was killed
3. are elections held
4. Mary was fired
5. Flights are sometimes cancelled
6. I was accused
7. was your sweater made
8. is not known by many people
9. the accident was caused

10. Was the first rocket sent
11. This letter is not pronounced the same
12. His shoes were covered with mud
13. Many houses are damaged

EXERCISE 55

2. painted by our handyman
3. be paid immediately
4. is being used by someone else
5. hasn't been cleaned (has not been cleaned) for weeks
6. is going to be built next year
7. is made from oil
8. was found nearby
9. be dry-cleaned
10. was being used by my secretary
11. have been called immediately
12. have been delivered

EXERCISE 56

3. worked
4. offered
5. was accepted
6. came
7. left
8. wasn't paid (was not paid)
9. complained
10. was done
11. asked
12. was refused
13. miss
14. promised
15. be reimbursed
16. be promoted
17. quit
18. be given
19. leaves

EXERCISE 57

2. c
3. k
4. b
5. f
6. l
7. i
8. a
9. d
10. g
11. e
12. j

EXERCISE 58

2. have a mole removed
3. have our telephone number changed
4. has her hair permed
5. have the brakes checked
6. have my teeth cleaned
7. have the prescription delivered

EXERCISE 59

A

3. T
4. F *Sample correction:* Most of her salary is spent because Julie buys lots of things in the store, and she has to spend a lot of money to repair her car.
5. T
6. F *Sample correction:* Julie's car has to be repaired often.
7. F *Sample correction:* Julie's college tuition won't be paid (will not be paid) by her parents. Julie is saving money for her tuition.

B

1. T
2. F *Sample correction:* Sally wasn't offered (was not offered) a scholarship. Her parents pay to send her to the boarding school.
3. F *Sample correction:* Sally wasn't given (was not given) her own room at the boarding school. She shares a room.
4. T
5. F *Sample correction:* Sally gets many invitations. She has many friends.

EXERCISE 60

1. he had to go to Toronto
2. [that] he didn't need (did not need); he had already read it
3. [that] his son was going to paint the house for him
4. [that] his family was doing well
5. [that] his father had been sick, but he was much better now
6. [that] he had really enjoyed your cookies
7. [that] he would see us next Saturday

EXERCISE 61

3. [that] he had a very nice accent in English *or* [that] he has . . .
4. to take it easy and relax
5. them [that] my brother was selling his house *or* . . . is selling his house
6. me to hold for a minute
7. me [that] I would have to help out more at home
8. [that] he had been very busy at work lately *or* [that] he has been . . .
9. me not to tell anyone what she had said *or* . . . what she said

10. I didn't have to bring (did not have to bring) a present to the birthday party *or* I don't have to bring (do not have to bring) . . .

EXERCISE 62

2. isn't (is not) very responsible about money
3. "He often spends money on himself instead of on me and the children."
4. don't tell (do not tell) your brother about our conversation."
5. "Don't worry (Do not worry). I won't say (will not say) anything."
6. "Speak to him frankly; but don't get (do not get) angry while you are discussing these matters."
7. "Anger will make him more reluctant to talk openly."
8. "I'll try (I will try) to follow your advice."

EXERCISE 63

3. [that] she always cut her hair herself; she didn't cut (did not cut)
4. [that] he always ate a very small breakfast, but he ate
5. [that] she was taking the bus to work Thursday morning, but she took her
6. [that] he didn't know (did not know) how to play a musical instrument, but I saw him play / playing
7. [that] she couldn't speak (could not speak) Spanish; spoke Spanish

EXERCISE 64

3. people came to your party [last weekend]?
4. do you miss a lot?
5. people were injured [in the traffic accident]?
6. good friends do you have?
7. left behind this toy?
8. is she studying
9. are you best friends
10. occurs twice a month?
11. did Roy lend you?
12. have you bought a house?
13. was your grandmother going to give you for your birthday?

EXERCISE 65

3. long have you had this car
4. Why didn't you go (did you not go) to work yesterday?
5. What are the children listening to?
6. What time are you getting up tomorrow? *or* What time are you going to get up . . .
7. How/Where can I find a good used car?
8. Aren't you feeling well?
9. What's (What is) your brother doing?
10. When did you come to this country?
11. How did you meet your husband?
12. Was your teacher born in this country?

13. Where were these clothes made?

EXERCISE 66

2. where the newspapers and magazines are
3. how much that chicken weighs
4. how far it is to San Francisco
5. when Shakespeare was born
6. why you got angry
7. what "diffident" means
8. where Ashgabad is

EXERCISE 67

2. when she was going to turn in the homework
3. The doctor asked Mr. Chen where he had pain.
4. Her boss asked Gloria whether she could stay late to do some work. *or* . . . if she could stay . . .
5. We asked the hotel clerk what time the bus went to the airport.
6. The travel agent asked Mrs. White whether she had ever been to Hawaii.
7. The patient asked the dentist whether it would hurt very much. *or* . . . if it would hurt . . .
8. I asked my friend on vacation in Florida how the weather was.
9. My father asked me why the police officer gave me a ticket.

EXERCISE 68

3. I haven't seen (have not seen) the new Canadian movie
4. I am very quiet
5. I shouldn't have (should not have) another piece of cake
6. My brother likes to cook
7. My friends didn't buy (did not buy) a present for Maria
8. Jeff had to take a business trip
9. Yesterday wasn't (was not) cold
10. My neighbors are on vacation
11. I can miss a day of work
12. Chris won't be (will not be) at the party
13. Sylvia's been (has been) to Brazil

EXERCISE 69

Answers will vary.
Sample answers:
4. So would I; I wouldn't; You would? I wouldn't.
5. So do I; She does? I don't.
6. Neither have I; You haven't? I have.
7. Neither did I; She didn't? I did.
8. Neither can I; You can't? I can.
9. So was I; You were? I wasn't.
10. Neither am I; You aren't? I am.
11. So should I.
12. So do I; He does? I don't.
13. So did I; You did? I didn't.
14. Neither was I; You weren't? I was.

EXERCISE 70

2. I think so.
3. I don't think (do not think) so.
4. I'm (I am) afraid so.
5. I'm (I am) afraid not.
6. I guess so.
7. I guess not.
8. I'm (I am) afraid not.
9. I don't think (do not think) so.
10. I hope not.
11. I suppose so.
12. I suppose not.
13. I hope so.

EXERCISE 71

A

2. can't you?
3. would you?
4. shouldn't it?
5. don't they?
6. would you?
7. isn't he?
8. didn't he?
9. doesn't he?
10. will you?

B

2. You weren't doing (were not doing) anything important
3. Hannah doesn't like (does not like) her new job
4. This shirt is expensive
5. I can use your tools
6. Your shirt wasn't made (was not made) in the United States
7. There isn't (is not) much milk left
8. You've finished (You have finished) your homework

EXERCISE 72

Answers will vary.

EXERCISE 73

2. doing the shopping
3. interrupting [me]
4. working in that
5. living alone
6. changing jobs until next year
7. watching a video at home
8. telling the same stories (over and over again) about his
9. driving his car as long as we buy some gas
10. lifting anything heavy until his back is better
11. walking to work every

EXERCISE 74

2. to get a raise
3. She; not to call him stupid
4. She; to give him a ride home
5. not to tell anyone what she said. *or* . . . what she had said
6. He; to visit his family for Christmas
7. not to buy a new car [right now]
8. He; to get a haircut
9. He; where to go on vacation; She; to help him decide
10. to have a day off
11. He; how to get to the airport at five in the morning [the next day]

EXERCISE 75

2. smoking
3. to pick
4. to eat
5. not playing
6. catching
7. to get; not to waste
8. grow
9. swimming; to fish
10. not to walk
11. do
12. to feed
13. studying
14. to stop; complaining
15. to give

EXERCISE 76

Sample answers:
3. buying *or* getting
4. laughing *or* smiling
5. working
6. putting *or* using
7. to pick up *or* to get
8. taking
9. to feel
10. meeting *or* talking to *or* speaking to
11. to drink
12. to calm down *or* to relax
13. to discuss

EXERCISE 77

2. h
3. l
4. k
5. b
6. i
7. j
8. f
9. d
10. g
11. a
12. e

5. eat at home than [eat] in a restaurant
6. drive other people's cars
7. stay home than go out
8. to Las Vegas
9. having their purchases delivered; carrying them home themselves
10. translated the letter into English
11. Are you going to call George; called him
12. didn't tell (did not tell) anyone what I said

EXERCISE 79

2. does Andrew expect to do well in school; making an effort
3. told me to improve my pronunciation; listening to native speakers
4. a lot to do; leaving town on business next week
5. having dinner at my favorite restaurant tonight
6. running five miles [every day]
7. going to a Japanese restaurant tonight
8. 's (is) lonely; making friends
9. Are you; going to Toronto next weekend
10. I found the restaurant; giving me directions
11. went to work this morning; having to drive on snow and ice

EXERCISE 80

3. sharing
4. living
5. remind
6. make
7. being
8. studying
9. drive
10. riding
11. taking
12. do
13. help
14. being
15. doing
16. letting

EXERCISE 81

Sample answers:
3. like going
4. of using *or* of borrowing *or* of driving
5. me for not being *or* . . . for not getting here
6. for forgetting *or* for not remembering
7. to giving *or* to presenting
8. on staying
9. in finding *or* in getting
10. from getting
11. her from going out with *or* from meeting *or* from seeing
12. of going
13. them from doing

14. on being
15. her of being

EXERCISE 82

3. apologizing [to people]
4. keeping that old magazine
5. [spending so much time] watching TV
6. driving across town just to buy lemons
7. calling Mary Jo
8. reaching my uncle by phone
9. shopping twice a week
10. inviting Emily to the party
11. hours fixing his car

EXERCISE 83

4. we wouldn't miss the bus
5. try on some shoes
6. lunch
7. she wouldn't forget (would not forget) to stop at the bank after work
8. he could get/buy some groceries
9. a trip to Finland
10. the employees would be able to spend the holiday with their families *or* . . . could spend the holiday . . .
11. be able to walk again

EXERCISE 84

A

2. to hear your brother finally got out of the hospital
3. to meet your parents the other night
4. to see you on TV last week
5. to learn that I didn't get the job

B

2. of you to think of others before yourself
3. of Carlos to go to bed with the doors open
4. of us to form an opinion of the woman before meeting her
5. of Maria to convince the police officer not to give her a ticket

C

2. to ask her father for money
3. of being turned down
4. to interrupt you
5. for interrupting your conversation this morning
6. in seeing that new Chinese movie
7. to know what you think of the movie

EXERCISE 85

Answers will vary.
Sample answers:
3. say
4. fall
5. coming *or* escaping

6. knocking
7. sing *or* play
8. wearing
9. eating
10. take
11. waiting
12. get
13. cooking
14. talking

EXERCISE 86

4. I had to wait a long time[,] sitting in agony.
5. The doctor gave me a prescription for a painkiller [,] promising it would work fast.
6. Not knowing that they would upset my stomach, I took the pills without food.
7. Having left me at the doctor's earlier, my friend came to my house to see me last night.
8. I woke up this morning[,] feeling much better.

EXERCISE 87

Answers will vary.
Sample answers:
1. The school can afford to buy new computers for the labs, and we'll be getting some in the next few months.
2. I can't help crying when I see a really sad movie.
3. I would rather eat at home than go to a restaurant.
4. The parents threatened to stop the child's allowance if she didn't get better grades.
5. I regret not doing my homework over the weekend.
6. His mother warned him not to spend all of his earnings on car payments.
7. Many prefer to work at home than to work in an office.
8. When I saw my friend for the first time in four years, we went on talking for five hours straight.
9. I can't stand being without my computer.
10. I don't mind waiting for ten minutes or fifteen minutes after a scheduled appointment time, but an hour is a long time to wait.
11. The employee denied taking the missing computer.
12. I pretended to listen to the lecture but I was doing a puzzle.
13. I can't imagine wearing a suit to work every day.
14. I must have mailed the letter, but I can't remember doing it.
15. Teens often try to act like adults before they are really adults.
16. The teacher advised Fred to work harder at his English pronunciation.
17. The teacher made the child do extra homework because the child wasn't doing well in math.
18. We are not allowed to use the parking places near the door.
19. I need to remember to buy some milk today.

20. I would like to have to choose between a vacation in Europe and a vacation in Hawaii.
21. My mother let me drive her car when I was sixteen.

EXERCISE 88

3. to visit
4. taking
5. getting
6. to decide
7. to go
8. leaving
9. studying
10. to know
11. to help
12. getting
13. feeling
14. to live
15. go
16. visiting
17. traveling

EXERCISE 89

Answers will vary.
Sample answers:
4. sleeping in a different bed
5. taking the bus to work; having to stand all the way
6. going straight home to bed
7. Dan; helping with the plans for my party
8. going to see the big soccer game
9. surfing the Internet
10. to the park and just walk around and relax
11. to throw their garbage on the sidewalk
12. to be alone at night
13. starting my own company
14. being impolite to a teacher
15. you play the piano
16. being good at repairs; fixing things around the house
17. studying for several hours; take a break and go for a walk

EXERCISE 90

Sample answers:
2. a. Black pepper, garlic, lemon juice, lettuce, mushrooms, oil, olives, pieces of onion, salt, and tomatoes
   b. Butter, jam, and bananas
3. a. Experience, a good coach, strong arms and legs, healthy lungs, and time to practice
   b. Long hair, rainy weather, and an umbrella
4. a. baby clothes, a good doctor, help from relatives, information about vaccinations, money, and a spare room
   b. a truck and new living room furniture
5. a. clean water, enough sleep, exercise, fresh air, and good food
   b. Alcohol, a car, coffee, an expensive doctor, a hard job, stress, and tobacco

EXERCISE 91

2. a suggestion
3. very good advice
4. Bad luck
5. bread
6. permission
7. a view
8. rooms
9. good progress; hard work
10. room; big suitcases
11. hair
12. luggage; a trip

EXERCISE 92

4. a
5. X
6. the
7. X
8. some
9. a
10. a
11. the
12. the
13. the
14. a
15. some
16. X
17. X
18. a
19. X
20. some
21. a
22. X
23. X
24. the
25. some
26. the
27. the
28. the
29. the
30. the
31. X
32. the
33. some
34. X
35. X
36. X
37. X
38. the

EXERCISE 93

2. the
3. X; X
4. X
5. The
6. X; X
7. the
8. X; X
9. X
10. X; X
11. The, the
12. X; the
13. X; the
14. X; X
15. X; X
16. the; the

EXERCISE 94

2. The Andes Mountains are; the Empire State Building
3. O'Hare Airport in Chicago is; the Rhine-Main Airport in Frankfurt
4. China has more people than India.
5. Mexico has a larger area than the Dominican Republic.
6. The north of Europe has a cooler climate than the south of Europe.
7. The Far East has a larger population than the Middle East.
8. The Nile River is longer than the Mississippi River.
9. Japan has a larger population than the Philippines.
10. The Great Wall of China is longer than the Suez Canal.
11. The Giza Pyramids were more difficult to build than Buckingham Palace.
12. Princeton University is more famous than the University of Arizona.

EXERCISE 95

4. Where are your binoculars?
5. My news is not so bad
6. Fifty dollars is a lot of money for a book.
7. only means of transportation is a bicycle
8. Is that TV series new or old?
9. The sharp scissors are not for children.
10. Mathematics is a difficult subject for many students.
11. are more police than firefighters in this city

EXERCISE 96

4. the beginning of the movie
5. back problems
6. My brother's back
7. the back of my hand
8. tonight's concert
9. cans of soda
10. soda cans
11. bottom of the boat
12. ocean fish
13. two-hour operation
14. the meaning of this word
15. money problems

EXERCISE 97

3. advice; is
4. furniture; needs
5. news; depresses
6. rooms; contain
7. Luggage; weighs
8. Noise; keeps
9. information; helps
10. hair; takes
11. vegetables; take
12. is; room

EXERCISE 98

    Two of my friends and I hope we can take 1 *a* trip to 2 ~~the~~ southern Mexico, Belize, and Guatemala this winter. I investigated 3 *the* cost of flights to those places, and it's pretty expensive, so I'm working with 4 *a* ~~the~~ travel agent to find 5 *the* lowest price. So far, the cheapest fare has been over $900, so we're still looking for 6 *a* ~~the~~ cheaper one.
    We would like to escape from 7 *the* ~~a~~ cold at home in Minnesota, visit some pyramids in 8 *the* area, spend some time at 9 *the* beach, and practice 10 ~~the~~ Spanish. Of course, we'll eat new dishes and meet 11 ~~the~~ new people, too. My friends think I am too interested in food, but that opinion is very unfair. In my opinion, the food in 12 *a* new country is just one part of 13 *the* culture of the country. To me, it would be a terrible mistake to go to 14 *a* foreign country and stay at fancy hotels and eat 15 *the* same food as at home.

EXERCISE 99

2. b
3. b
4. a
5. b
6. a
7. a

EXERCISE 100

4. myself; X
5. themselves
6. X
7. each other
8. themselves
9. ourselves
10. herself
11. each other
12. yourself
13. themselves; X
14. yourselves; each other
15. yourself *or* yourselves

EXERCISE 101

2. him
3. their own
4. them
5. their
6. his own
7. his
8. himself
9. his own
10. him
11. mine
12. his
13. his own

EXERCISE 102

2. is no high school *or* isn't (is not) a high school
3. There is; on this road
4. There was; the airport
5. There is a lot of; my coffee
6. didn't (did not) eat because there wasn't (was not)
7. There might be a party; next week
8. There; be a stop sign at that corner
9. There is; noise here; work

EXERCISE 103

3. It's (It is) too far [to drive].
4. there isn't (is not) any cream *or* there's (there is) not any cream
5. It wasn't (was not) nice enough
6. There's (There is) something wrong with it.
7. It's (It is) wonderful
8. There's (There is) a light
9. It's (It is) too late to stop by
10. There's (There is) not enough for everyone.
11. It was very interesting.
12. There was a lot of flu at work last year.
13. There was a lot of snow there last winter.

EXERCISE 104

3. someone
4. anywhere
5. something
6. anyone
7. someone
8. any
9. someone
10. Anyone
11. anything

2. 'm (am) not doing anything
3. No one; didn't tell (did not tell) anyone
4. Nowhere; aren't going (are not going) anywhere
5. None; don't owe (do not owe) me any money
6. Nothing; didn't say (did not say) anything about
7. Nowhere; don't want (do not want) to go anywhere [tomorrow]
8. None; doesn't have (does not have) any free time
9. No one; didn't give (did not give) money to anyone
10. None; didn't invite (did not invite) any people to the party
11. No one; didn't invite (did not invite) anyone to the party

EXERCISE 106

2. none
3. any
4. No
5. any
6. None
7. no

EXERCISE 107

3. My brother spends a lot of time fixing his car.
4. We won't have trouble finding a place to stay in Los Angeles. There are plenty of hotels there.
5. Martha is a lucky woman. She has few enemies.
6. Right
7. Josh has lots of clothes. Why does he need to borrow yours?
8. My grandparents are very active. They go out a lot.
9. Mr. James isn't a very good boss. He has little patience.
10. Right
11. There aren't many reasons to visit that town unless you like old mines.
12. I ate a few hours ago, but I'm hungry again.

EXERCISE 108

3. most days
4. both presents *or* both of the presents
5. both of them
6. either of his brothers
7. either author
8. both days
9. Some days
10. Neither of the presents
11. some money; a few dollars
12. neither city
13. neither of them

EXERCISE 109

3. Neither of
4. Both [of]
5. Neither of
6. either of
7. None of
8. Neither
9. Neither of; both [of]
10. All [of]
11. None of
12. all [of]

EXERCISE 110

3. whole
4. Everyone
5. whole
6. Every *or* Each
7. each *or* every
8. everyone
9. All
10. all

EXERCISE 111

Answers will vary.
Sample answers:
1. I have a lot of homework, so I don't have much time to watch TV.
2. I have two aunts in Russia, but I have never seen either of them.
3. I like most science fiction movies, but I don't have time to see many of them.
4. Very few people go through life without a little help from friends.
5. Most of my friends are attending college, and about half of them are graduating this year.
6. Peter didn't talk to any of his friends about his family, and none of them knew he had a brother.
7. My brothers are both lawyers, but neither of them is a trial lawyer who argues in court.
8. No one I know plays hockey, but some people I know ice-skate.
9. My brother has plenty of CDs, but he never lends any of them to anyone.

EXERCISE 112

4. I can depend on in an emergency
5. I left for you on the table
6. who gave him a lot of help after class
7. who he liked the best
8. we met on vacation
9. you're pointing to
10. I like
11. you went to school with
12. who *or* that used to live next door

EXERCISE 113

3. Do you know the name of the song (which) we just listened to?
4. *Who* is necessary
5. Did you call the woman (who) you wanted to talk to?
6. Sylvia hasn't seen the people (that) she used to work with for years
7. *That* is necessary
8. Have you eaten all the food (that) we bought together?
9. *That* is necessary
10. *That* is necessary
11. Did you see anyone (that) we know at the party?
12. *That* is necessary
13. My brother hates the movie star (that) I was just watching on TV
14. *Who* is necessary
15. The people (who) you live with are very nice

EXERCISE 114

5. [that/why] she wants a bigger house
6. [that] they got married
7. who wants to be a soccer player when she grows up
8. whose wife and daughter are both police officers
9. that/why; is moving to a new apartment
10. where people get passports
11. whom; sold his car
12. [that] they went to Alaska

EXERCISE 115

2. The ostrich, which can't fly, can run very fast.
3. Eagles, which have sharp beaks and very good sight, hunt and eat small animals.
4. Americans sometimes compare a foolish or stubborn person to a donkey, which is an animal in the horse family with short legs and long ears.
5. I have always been fascinated by camels, which are known to travel long distances without water.
6. Elephants, whose tusks are made into ivory jewelry and decorations, are protected in many countries.
7. Elephants are once again being killed by hunters, many of whom hunt illegally.
8. The kangaroo carries its young in its pouch, which is like a big pocket made of skin.
9. Goats, which have a reputation for eating anything, live wild in mountain areas or are kept on farms.
10. Many people, most of whom haven't seen dangerous animals, are afraid of animals like rattlesnakes and sharks.
11. The llama, whose wool is soft and expensive, is at home in the Andes Mountains of South America.
12. Some swimmers are afraid of dolphins, which is surprising because they are intelligent, friendly animals.

EXERCISE 116

A

3. hoping to get scholarships
4. interviewed last week
5. The company employing 250 workers
6. The workers employed at the mine
7. The job offering more benefits
8. The students confused by the homework

B

3. hoping to get scholarships need to get good
4. interviewed last week got the job
5. employing 250 workers is going to close
6. The workers employed at the mine went on strike.

EXERCISE 117

Answers will vary.
Sample answers:

3. I would like to meet Isabel Allende, who is a well-known writer.
4. The president of the United States is a person whose job is very difficult. I wouldn't like to have it.
5. I was given a ticket to the concert by someone I met waiting in line.
6. A big house is something I've always wanted.
7. People who criticize others usually have a lot of faults themselves.
8. A friend gave me this CD, which has a lot of my favorite songs on it.
9. I visited the museum with Edna, with whom I always have a good time.
10. One day I want to visit Africa, where my mother was born.
11. The park is always a place where I can relax.
12. I have two sisters, both of whom are married.
13. I have two cars, neither of which is working.
14. I have been a friend of Diana's from the day that I met her.

EXERCISE 118

3. 's (is) disgusted
4. was depressing
5. was upsetting
6. 's (is) interested
7. were; disappointed
8. are; confusing
9. 're (are) excited
10. was amusing
11. was embarrassed
12. 'll be freezing (will be freezing)
13. were; surprising

EXERCISE 119

2. beautiful big old stone
3. 's (is) a typical sixteen-year-old city

4. has a big old blue German
5. a cute brown and grey
6. favorite traditional Mexican
7. great new Thai
8. spent her money / on gorgeous old Central Asian
9. nice young foreign
10. bought modern black and white steel

EXERCISE 120

3. incredibly quickly
4. really fluent
5. very slowly
6. very strange for some reason
7. the dress carefully before buying it
8. continuously for three days
9. seriously injured in the accident
10. surprisingly quickly from her accident
11. cold and brief
12. The situation; very serious

EXERCISE 121

5. late
6. hard
7. well
8. fast
9. hardly
10. fast
11. well
12. hardly
13. well
14. good

EXERCISE 122

A

3. have so much food at home
4. has such a bad cold
5. was so cold
6. was so busy
7. 'm having (am having) such a good time
8. had such a big breakfast

B

3. so much food at home that I don't want (do not want) to go out to eat tonight
4. such a bad cold that she's going to stay (she is going to stay) home from work tomorrow
5. was so cold that I didn't walk (did not walk) to work this morning
6. so busy that I didn't say (did not say) goodbye to him last night
7. 'm having (am having) such a good time that I don't want (do not want) to go home
8. such a big breakfast that I'm skipping (I am skipping) lunch today

EXERCISE 123

A

2. Mrs. Garcia isn't healthy enough to live by herself.
3. The jacket was too small for Millie to wear.
4. Josh isn't old enough to drive a car.
5. George is too nice to do such a terrible thing.
6. Do you have enough money to lend me some?
7. I can't type fast enough to finish this report on time.
8. Is there enough water to support life on Mars?

B

2. Mrs. Garcia is; to live by herself
3. The jacket wasn't (was not) big enough for Millie to wear.
4. Josh is too young to drive a car.
5. George isn't (is not) mean enough to do such a terrible thing.

EXERCISE 124

3. more modern
4. cheaper
5. better
6. thinner
7. easier
8. more interesting
9. earlier
10. larger
11. more loudly
12. harder
13. safer
14. more carefully
15. friendlier
16. worse

EXERCISE 125

1. A: more
   B: a little
   A: The; more
2. A: any
   B: better
   A: more
   B: more; faster
   A: more, the
3. B: the sooner
   A: sooner; better
   B: faster; much

EXERCISE 126

3. eat as much fish
4. more free time
5. feel as well today
6. talk as much as
7. drives farther to work than
8. to be friendlier
9. answer the question as intelligently as I expected

10. as many people at the game as usual
11. as happy as she seems
12. more comfortable than they look

EXERCISE 127

3. of the busiest people
4. the best coffee
5. the oldest child in his family
6. of the most expensive cities in Europe
7. the nicest hotel in the city
8. the most famous person
9. the most pleasant season of the year
10. of the best teams in the country
11. the safest form of transportation

EXERCISE 128

2. has probably burned his lunch again
3. almost forgot your birthday last week
4. Mr. Lee can only walk with a cane
5. Mrs. Conrad don't usually travel abroad in the winter
6. likes to drink hot chocolate at her desk every morning
7. never has time to go hiking on the weekends
8. like your new suit and overcoat a lot *or* like your new overcoat and suit . . .
9. is seldom in her apartment on Saturday
10. forgot your glasses at my house last night
11. will definitely get to work on time next week
12. also sings with his friends in a choir on the weekend

EXERCISE 129

3. isn't (is not) a dry cleaner's anymore
4. still are lots of cars on Main Street
5. don't ride (do not ride) their bikes on Main Street anymore
6. aren't able to go (are not able to go) to the movies on Main Street anymore *or* can't go . . .
7. still have trouble parking downtown
8. can still find something to read in town

EXERCISE 130

3. I'm ^ waiting for my brother to call. *(still)*
4. You haven't said anything ^. *(yet)*
5. she ^ knew about your accident. *(already)*
6. He ^ jogs pretty often. *(still)*
7. Has she decided if she is coming to dinner with us ^? *(yet)*
8. I don't eat there ^ . *(anymore)*
9. I've ^ started cooking dinner. *(already)*

10. Do you ^ want to drive. *(still)*
11. I'm ^ not ready to do it. *or* I'm not ready to do it ^ . *(still / yet)*
12. she ^ has one. *(already)*
13. His clothes don't fit him ^. *(anymore)*
14. I ^ have a few things to do. *(still)*
15. Do you ^ go hiking on the weekends like before? *(still)*
    No, we don't have time ^. *(anymore)*

EXERCISE 131

2. even
3. even though
4. even
5. Even though
6. even
7. even
8. even if
9. even
10. even though

EXERCISE 132

Answers will vary.
Sample answers:
1. You have to work hard to be able to speak English well; learning it well doesn't happen quickly or without effort.
2. Louisa described the film perfectly when she said that it was long and boring.
3. The South American rain forests have some unusual plants and animals, as well as some incredibly beautiful ones.
4. The black fox moved quietly through the dead branches, hunting its prey.
5. I am in interested in ancient silver, but I am hardly an expert on it.
6. Happily, I haven't received any disappointing news lately.
7. I got to work surprisingly late even though I drove fast.
8. Sadly, my friend feels very lonely in the big city, but at least he is satisfied with his new job.

EXERCISE 133

3. It takes Kevin longer to get home because he doesn't live as near work as I do.
4. I'm staying home from school because my cold is worse today than it was yesterday.

5. Sam bought the beige rug because it didn't cost as <u>much</u> as the blue one.
6. Everyone would like to be married to the <u>nicest</u> person in the world.
7. A friend of mine lost his job because he wasn't as <u>hardworking</u> as his coworkers.
8. New technology is making cars <u>safer and safer</u>
9. Coffee and tea are among the <u>cheapest</u> beverages in the world.
10. As time goes by, computers are becoming <u>cheaper</u> and <u>more</u> common.
11. Fred can wear my clothes because he's the <u>same</u> size <u>as</u> me.

EXERCISE 134

4. the richest person in
5. as badly as
6. harder than
7. more slowly than
8. A. bigger
   B. the most populous country in
9. as nice as
10. A. easier
    B. the easiest
11. A. worse than
    B. as much as
12. A. as often as;
    B. busier than

EXERCISE 135

Answers will vary.
Sample answers:
1. I don't have as much work this week as I did last week.
2. The more time he spends with his family, the happier he is.
3. This house isn't as expensive as the other one we looked at, but it needs more repairs.
4. The more I tried to clean the spot on my shirt, the bigger it got.
5. This is the most expensive meal I've ever eaten.
6. The happiest day of my life will be when I finish school.
7. I have the same job title as Sandra, but I make a lot less money.
8. I am a lot busier than I used to be now that I have a baby.
9. As I was looking for my lost wallet, I got more and more upset.
10. We fished for a longer time than they did, but we didn't catch as many fish as they did.

EXERCISE 136

4. sick, my sister had to take care of my nephew
5. I didn't care for the lunch my aunt made, I ate it anyway

6. I wasn't very busy yesterday. I forgot to go to the bank
7. my sister had a flu shot, she still got the flu
8. answer, Angela didn't show any anger herself
9. the United States spends more on health care than Canada, it doesn't have a better health care system
10. I wasn't very hungry. I went to a restaurant with my friends
11. having problems with her teenagers; manages to stay in a good mood

EXERCISE 137

2. lose her job unless she is rude to customers
3. You should take extra money along on your trip in case you need it in San Francisco
4. The Suarez teenagers can stay out late as long as they call home to say where they are
5. 'll go (will go) running unless it's raining (it is raining) in the morning
6. Ted always leaves his phone number with the baby-sitter in case she needs to contact him
7. 'll get along with (will get along with) Angela as long as you are careful what you say to her
8. I can go to the movies with you providing you pay my way
9. don't you take your allergy medicine along in case you need it
10. My computer printer usually works well if I haven't been using (have not been using) it too much
11. I have enough money; go to Hawaii with you

EXERCISE 138

2. As
3. as if
4. as
5. like
6. when
7. As
8. like
9. Since
10. like
11. as
12. as though
13. as if
14. like
15. as
16. like
17. as if
18. like
19. as if
20. as if
21. as
22. as

EXERCISE 139

2. g
3. e
4. a
5. c
6. b
7. f

EXERCISE 140

2. for
3. While
4. for
5. for
6. while
7. until
8. for
9. until
10. by
11. During
12. until
13. by
14. By the time

EXERCISE 141

Answers will vary.
Sample answers:
1. Even though my car was old, I was able to sell it for a fairly good price.
2. In spite of all my hard work, I didn't get a raise this year.
3. I packed some extra sweaters in case the weather gets cold.
4. My parents don't get angry with me unless I do something really wrong or really dangerous.
5. As long as I'm happy in this job, I'll stay in it.
6. I will probably go to the big concert provided I have enough money for a ticket.
7. As I get older, I now realize that my parents were often right.
8. Like most people, I want to have at least one good friend.
9. Sometimes I feel as though my job takes up too much of my time.
10. We painted the old furniture, and now it looks as if it were new.

EXERCISE 142

1. b. on
   c. in
2. a. in
   b. X
3. a. at
   b. in; at
   c. X
4. a. in
   b. in

c. at
d. In
e. in
5. a. on
   b. in
   c. on
6. a. At; in
   b. at; at
   c. X

EXERCISE 143

2. in; at
3. at; at
4. at *or* in
5. at; on
6. at; in; on
7. at; at
8. at; on
9. in; in
10. on
11. in; at *or* in
12. in
13. on; on
14. on; in
15. on; on
16. in
17. on
18. on; in

EXERCISE 144

2. in my car; by bus
3. by someone with a stone
4. by check; in cash
5. with a very good camera by a professional
6. on TV by countless people
7. by accident; on purpose
8. in/by my car; on the five o'clock train
9. by hand by my aunt
10. by the American writer Arthur Miller on the radio

EXERCISE 145

2. arrived at the hotel early
3. go in my car
4. were away on vacation last week
5. 's (is) cheaper and faster to go by subway
6. I went on my bike
7. 've never been (have never been) to Florida
8. can't get into her small car
9. went to bed late last night
10. fixed it with glue

EXERCISE 146

3. the damage to many buildings is extensive
4. The cause of their argument isn't (is not) clear to me.
5. There's (There is) an urgent need for blankets and clothes.

186 ANSWER KEY

6. it isn't (is not) easy to find a solution to the problem
7. don't know (do not know) the answer to that question
8. His relationship with his father isn't (is not) very good

EXERCISE 147

2. ashamed of
3. jealous of
4. satisfied with
5. responsible for
6. generous to
7. silly of
8. capable of
9. worried about
10. different than/from

EXERCISE 148

3. am; of people who talk too much
4. was; of milk
5. My problem is; to yours
6. Joy is; of dogs
7. I'm (I am); for yelling at you yesterday
8. My Brazilian friend is; of fruit
9. Linda is; with school
10. Our teacher is; of students who come late to class
11. isn't (is not); at playing baseball

EXERCISE 149

2. shouted; at
3. talk to
4. taking care of
5. looked for
6. explain to
7. throw; at
8. apologized to
9. care for
10. care; about
11. invite; to
12. explain; to
13. asking; for
14. applied to

EXERCISE 150

3. your house to me
4. about it
5. for them
6. about your problem
7. for the airport
8. when we eat
9. to the doctor how he felt
10. to what I'm saying
11. at a used car
12. about your appearance
13. for Jason
14. to us why he didn't vote
15. her problem to the teacher
16. after himself

EXERCISE 151

2. me of someone I know
3. Amy complained; for her car
4. from Hannah since last summer
5. More Americans; from heart disease than from cancer
6. of moving to San Francisco
7. me of being lazy
8. That child; on cereal and milk
9. This sunscreen; from
10. (people) about serious weather conditions
11. of the name of that restaurant
12. me for your

EXERCISE 152

2. o
3. j
4. a
5. n
6. g
7. b
8. k
9. m
10. c
11. p
12. l
13. f
14. e
15. i
16. h

EXERCISE 153

2. tried them on
3. see me off
4. wake them up
5. show us around
6. looked them up
7. put it out
8. threw it away
9. break it down
10. filling them out

EXERCISE 154

2. fill out
3. throw; away/out
4. gave; away
5. get by
6. showed up
7. making; up
8. drops out
9. turn; down
10. dozes off
11. calm down
12. crossed; out
13. keep; up

EXERCISE 155

Answers will vary.
Sample answers:

1. In the last century, inventions changed people's lives, and I'm sure inventions will continue to do the same in the future.
2. On weekdays we always have supper at the same time, but on weekends our schedule is more flexible.
3. We thought that we were going to be late for class, but in the end the teacher didn't show up at all.
4. On nice days the children play in the yard, but on some days bad weather forces them to play in the house.
5. In my opinion, judges and jurors should review the evidence carefully before they send anyone to prison.
6. Will was riding on a bicycle when he hit a bump and fell off. Now he's in the hospital.
7. On the way to the store, I ran into an old friend by accident and we had a nice chat.
8. In most countries in the world, people drive on the right.
9. We can eat our picnic food either sitting on the ground or sitting at a table.
10. Alan didn't forget the tickets on purpose. On the whole, I think you're being unreasonable by being so angry about it.

EXERCISE 156

Answers will vary.
Sample answers:

1. school expenses
2. hiding the truth
3. leave the car doors unlocked
4. my friends; I need good advice
5. becoming a well-known writer
6. many other students; don't have a full-time job
7. classical music
8. my relatives in Poland
9. the high number of unemployed people
10. the poor in our society
11. playing tennis
12. my friend Liz; she really listens to me and understands me
13. my ability to speak English.